Zaner-Bloser
Handwriting
With a new alphabet

Author

Clinton S. Hackney

Contributing Authors

Pamela J. Farris

Janice T. Jones

Linda Leonard Lamme

WITHDRAWN

Todd Wehr
Memorial Library

Zaner-Bloser, Inc., P.O. Box 16764, Columbus, Ohio 43216-6764   1-800-421-3018

Developed by Kirchoff/Wohlberg, Inc., in cooperation with Zaner-Bloser Publishers

Printed in the United States of America

98 99 WC 5 4

You already know handwriting is important.
Now take a look at...

NEW
Zaner-Bloser Handwriting

Easier to read!   Easier to write!   Easier to teach!

I see Zaner-Bloser's
alphabet in the books I read.

I like Zaner-Bloser because
it's so easy to write.

Zaner-Bloser's new
program is easy to teach.

ii

You already know handwriting is important, but did you know...

Did You Know...

Annually, the U.S. Postal Service receives 38 million illegibly addressed letters, costing American taxpayers $4 million each year.

–American Demographics, Dec. 1992

Did You Know...

Hundreds of thousands of tax returns are delayed every year because figures, notes, and signatures are illegible.

–Better Handwriting in 30 Days, 1989

Did You Know...

Poor handwriting costs American business $200 million annually.

–American Demographics, Dec. 1992

Zaner-Bloser's CONTINUOUS-STROKE manuscript alphabet

Aa Bb Cc Dd Ee Ff Gg
Oo Pp Qq Rr Ss Tt

Easier to Read

Our vertical manuscript alphabet is like the alphabet kids see every day inside and outside of the classroom. They see it in their school books, in important environmental print like road signs, and in books and cartoons they read for fun.

"[Slanted] manuscript is not only harder to learn than traditional [vertical] print, but it creates substantially more letter recognition errors and causes more letter confusion than does the traditional style."

–Debby Kuhl and Peter Dewitz in a paper presented at the 1994 meeting of the American Educational Research Association

Please, my friends, a moment of silence, as the flying Zucchinis attempt a twisting triple somersault.

CALIFORNIA LIN 216

STOP

Vertical manuscript is the alphabet we see every day.

CIRCUS by Lois Ehlert ©1992 by Lois Ehlert

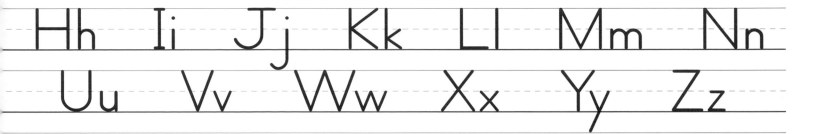

Easier to Write

Our vertical manuscript alphabet is written with continuous strokes—fewer pencil lifts—so there's a greater sense of flow in writing. And kids can write every letter once they learn four simple strokes that even kindergartners can manage.

Four simple strokes: circle, horizontal line, vertical line, slanted line

"The writing hand has to change direction more often when writing the [slanted] alphabet, do more retracing of lines, and make more strokes that occur later in children's development."

–Steve Graham in *Focus on Exceptional Children*, 1992

Many kids can already write their names when they start school (vertical manuscript).

Kirk

Why should they have to relearn them in another form (slanted manuscript)? With Zaner-Bloser, they don't have to.

Kirk

Easier to Teach

Our vertical manuscript alphabet is easy to teach because there's no reteaching involved. Children are already familiar with our letterforms—they've seen them in their environment and they've learned them at home.

"Before starting school, many children learn how to write traditional [vertical] manuscript letters from their parents or preschool teachers. Learning a special alphabet such as [slanted] means that these children will have to relearn many of the letters they can already write."

–Steve Graham in *Focus on Exceptional Children*, 1992

Zaner-Bloser's NEW SIMPLIFIED cursive alphabet

Aa Bb Cc Dd Ee Ff Gg

Nn Oo Pp Qq Rr Ss

Simplified letterforms...
Easier to read and write

old letterform

Letterforms are simplified so they're easier to write and easier to identify in writing. The new simplified **Q** now looks like a **Q** instead of a number 2.

old letterform

Our simplified letterforms use the headline, midline, and baseline as a guide for where letters start and stop. The new simplified **d** touches the headline instead of stopping halfway.

old letterform

No more "cane stems!" Our new simplified letterforms begin with a small curve instead of fancy loops that can be difficult for students to write.

Hh Ii Jj Kk Ll Mm
Tt Uu Vv Ww Xx Yy Zz

Simplified letterforms...
Easier to teach

When handwriting is easy for students to write, instruction time is cut way back! That's the teaching advantage with Zaner-Bloser Handwriting. Our cursive letterforms are simplified so instead of spending a lot of time teaching fancy loops that give kids trouble, teachers give instruction for simple, basic handwriting that students can use for the rest of their lives.

These simple letters are so much easier to teach!

And remember, with Zaner-Bloser Handwriting, students learn to write manuscript with continuous strokes. That means that when it's time for those students to begin writing cursive, the transition comes naturally because they already know the flow of continuous strokes.

The Student Edition...set up for student success

Letters are grouped and taught by the strokes used to form them.

Letter models show stroke direction and sequence.

Students first practice letters, then joinings, and finally complete words and sentences.

Students evaluate their own handwriting in every lesson.

Write Doublecurve and Overcurve Letters

T, F, I, and *Q* are not joined to the letter that follows.
J is joined to the letter that follows.

Write the letters, joinings, and words. Then write the sentences.

T	T	Texas	Tyler
F	F	Florida	Fort Lee
I	I	Iowa	Independence
Q	Q	Queensland	Quincy
J	J	Ju	Ja	Jo
Juneau	Jamaica	Joplin

DID YOU KNOW?

Texas chose the first state tree.

The oak is Iowa's state tree.

EVALUATE Circle your best word.

24

Grade 5 Student Edition

Language arts connections are easy with activities like this one. Here students learn about punctuation marks and then use them as they practice their handwriting.

Write Punctuation Marks

Use these punctuation marks to help clarify your writing.

. period	? question mark	! exclamation point
, comma	' apostrophe	" quotation marks

Write each sentence in cursive. Remember to slant punctuation marks.

"I'm thirsty," Sarah whined.

"She's bothering me!" Sam complained.

"Settle down back there!" Dad ordered.

"Are we there yet?" I asked.

On Your Own Write a sentence with at least three punctuation marks.

EVALUATE Are your question mark and exclamation point the correct size?   Yes   No

37

Grade 5 Student Edition

Write Lead Sentences

A lead sentence is the first sentence of a story. It may tell *who, what, when,* and *where.* Sometimes it tells *why.*

James Wilson Marshall | *discovered gold*
who | what

at Sutter's Mill | *this morning.*
where | when

Use the facts to write lead sentences.

Who: *Mrs. O'Leary's cow*   Where: *in the O'Leary barn*
What: *kicked over a lantern*   When: *last night*

_____

_____

Who: *Abolitionist Sojourner Truth*

What: *spoke*   When: *yesterday*

Where: *at Seneca Falls*   Why: *to get voting rights*

_____

_____

_____

On Your Own Write a lead sentence about either a school event or a historical event. Try to include the five W's: *who, what, when, where,* and *why.*

_____

_____

EVALUATE Is there space for *O* between letters?   Yes   No

53

Grade 5 Student Edition

Students learn to appreciate diverse cultures through activities like this one, in which they write time in Spanish.

Write in Spanish

What time is it?   *¿Qué hora es?*
It is 1:00.   *Es la una.*
It is 2:00.   *Son las dos.*
2:15   *dos y cuarto*
2:30   *dos y media*
2:45   *tres menos cuarto*

Write the time in Spanish. Use the word and number keys to help you.

1 una   *4 cuatro*   *7 siete*   *10 diez*
2 dos   *5 cinco*   *8 ocho*   *11 once*
3 tres   *6 seis*   *9 nueve*   *12 doce*

1. **6:00**   2. **5:15**   3. **7:45**   4. **11:15**   5. **10:30**

1. *Son las seis.* _____

2. _____

3. _____

4. _____

5. _____

On Your Own ¿Qué hora es? Answer in Spanish to the nearest quarter hour. _____

EVALUATE Are all your short letters the same size?   Yes   No

41

Grade 5 Student Edition

ix

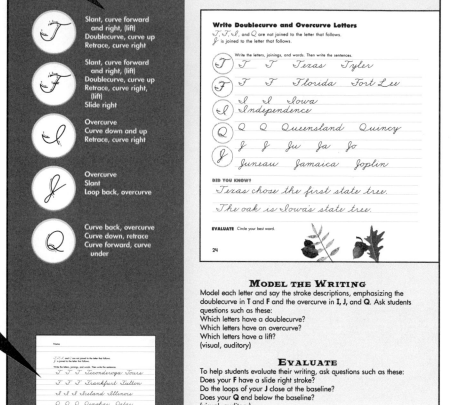

Slant, curve forward
and right, (lift)
Doublecurve, curve up
Retrace, curve right

Slant, curve forward
and right, (lift)
Doublecurve, curve up
Retrace, curve right,
(lift)
Slide right

Overcurve
Curve down and up
Retrace, curve right

Overcurve
Slant
Loop back, overcurve

Curve back, overcurve
Curve down, retrace
Curve forward, curve
under

Grade 5 Teacher Edition

Write Doublecurve and Overcurve Letters

T, F, I, and Q are not joined to the letter that follows.
J is joined to the letter that follows.

Write the letters, joinings, and words. Then write the sentences.

T   T   T   Texas   Tyler
F   F   F   Florida   Fort Lee
I   I   I   Iowa
Independence
Q   Q   Q   Queensland   Quincy
J   J   J   Ju   Ja   Jo
Juneau   Jamaica   Joplin

DID YOU KNOW?
Texas chose the first state tree.
The oak is Iowa's state tree.

EVALUATE Circle your best word.

24

MODEL THE WRITING
Model each letter and say the stroke descriptions, emphasizing the doublecurve in **T** and **F** and the overcurve in **I**, **J**, and **Q**. Ask students questions such as these:
Which letters have a doublecurve?
Which letters have an overcurve?
Which letters have a lift?
(visual, auditory)

EVALUATE
To help students evaluate their writing, ask questions such as these:
Does your **F** have a slide right stroke?
Do the loops of your **J** close at the baseline?
Does your **Q** end below the baseline?
(visual, auditory)

Joining Alert
Joining **T**, **F**, and **I** to the letter that follows is optional.

At-a-glance stroke descriptions are short and easy to find.

Visual references to practice masters for each lesson save you time.

Brief teaching notes save you valuable time.

x

The student page is
close to the instruction for
that page.

Write Lead Sentences

A lead sentence is the first sentence of a story. It may tell who, what, when, and where. Sometimes it tells why.

James Wilson Marshall discovered gold,
who   what

at Sutter's Mill, this morning.
where   when

Use the facts to write lead sentences.

Who: *Mrs. O'Leary's cow*   Where: *in the O'Leary barn*

_____

_____

Who: *Abolitionist Sojourner Truth*
What: *spoke*   When: *yesterday*
Where: *at Seneca Falls*   Why: *to get voting rights*

_____

_____

On Your Own Write a lead sentence about either a school event or a historical event. Try to include the five W's: who, what, when, where, and why.

EVALUATE Is there space for *O* between letters?   Yes   No

53

EVALUATE

After students have evaluated the spacing between their letters, ask if their writing is legible. Have them explain why or why not. (visual, auditory)

BEFORE WRITING
Share with students lead sentences of articles in a newspaper. Discuss which of the five *W*'s (*who, what, when, where,* and *why*) are covered by the story leads.

KEYS TO LEGIBILITY: CORRECT SPACING
Remind students that shifting their papers as they write can help keep spacing consistent. (visual, kinesthetic)

WRITE AWAY
Ask students to complete the story they began on page 53. Point out that in the process of writing, students may want to revise their story leads.

Language arts
connections reinforce writing
and other skills.

53

Grade 5 Teacher Edition

Grade 5 Practice Masters

An accompanying book of practice masters offers additional practice for every letter and skill students learn. It also includes resources to make teaching easier—certificates, an evaluation record, letters to send home to keep parents and guardians involved, and Spanish activities.

xi

Evaluation and Assessment...
consistent guidance throughout the year

Student self-evaluation...

In every lesson. Students evaluate their own handwriting and circle their best work.

In every review. Several times a year, students review the letterforms and joinings they've learned and again evaluate their handwriting.

Through application activities. Students apply what they've learned in relevant practice activities that fill half the book. In each activity, they evaluate their own handwriting.

Teacher assessment...

In every lesson and review. As students evaluate their own writing, teachers can assess their letterforms, as well as their comprehension of good handwriting. Corrective Strategies for each lesson offer teachers helpful hints for common handwriting problems.

Through application activities. Students' work in relevant practice activities offers lots of opportunity for informal assessment of handwriting, language arts, and other areas.

The Keys to Legibility

These four Keys to Legibility are taught and reviewed throughout the program.
They remind students that their goal should be legible handwriting.

Size

Consistently sized letters are easy to read. Students learn to write letterforms that are consistent in size.

Slant

Letters with a consistent slant are easy to read. Students learn how to position their papers and hold their pencils so consistent slant comes with ease.

Shape

Four simple strokes—undercurve, downcurve, overcurve, and slant—make it easy for students to write letters with consistent and proper shape.

Spacing

Correct spacing between letters and words makes handwriting easy to read. Practical hints show students how to determine correct spacing.

Handwriting practice...relevant application

Write Quickly

Practice writing quickly. Choose one of these sayings from Ben Franklin's *Poor Richard's Almanack* or a favorite saying of your own. Write the sentence as many times as you can in one minute. At the same time, try to write legibly.

Fish and visitors smell in three days.
If your head is wax, don't walk in the su
A small leak will sink a great ship.

LEGIBLE LETTERS

Do not draw your letters.
Write smoothly.

See you later, alligator!
See you later, alligator!
See you later, alligator!
See you later, alligator!
See you later, alligator!
See you later, alligator!
See you later, alligator!

EVALUATE Can you read your writing easily? (Yes)
Can a friend read it? (Yes)

34

**Completed Grade 5
Student Edition**

> Students practice writing quickly and legibly, so their handwriting is very functional in the real world.

Edit Your Writing

Use these proofreading marks to edit your writing.

≡ Capitalize.   ∧ Insert (add).
/ Use lowercase.   ⤸ Delete (take out).
⊙ Add period.   ¶ Indent for paragraph.

Write this paragraph correctly. Make the changes indicated by the proofreading marks.

¶ *You can have a good time at a museum. Just follow these Rules. Eat something food before you go. wear comfortable shoes. Don't try to see everything! Just pick exhibits that interest you⊙*

Anyone can have a good time at a museum. Just follow these rules. Eat something before you go. Wear comfortable shoes. Don't try to see everything! Just pick one or two exhibits that interest you.

EVALUATE Does your writing have uniform slant? (Yes) No

46

> In this practice activity, students learn how to edit and rewrite a paragraph.

A huge collection of supplementary materials...
makes handwriting even easier to teach!

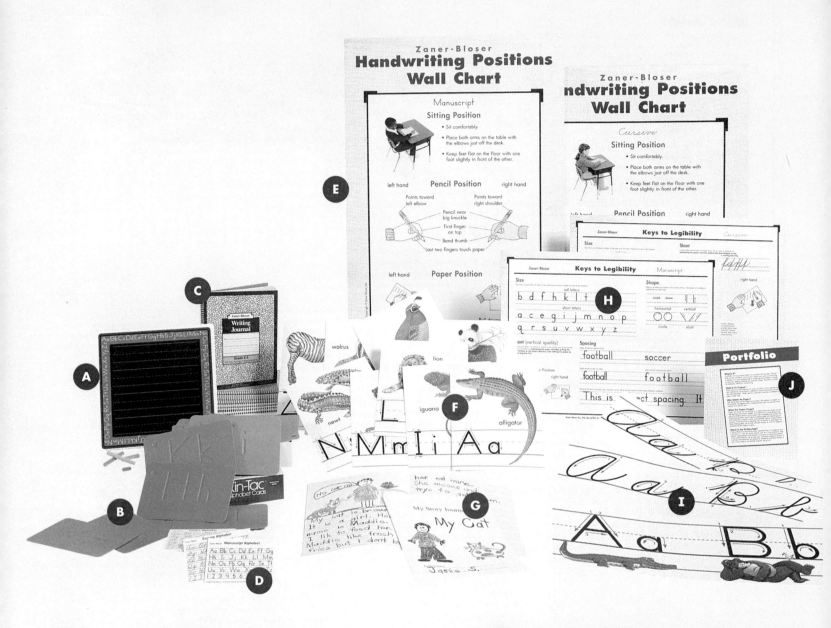

A **Practice Chalkboards** *grades K–4*

B **Manuscript Kin-Tac Cards** *grades K–2*

C **Writing Journals** *grades 1–6*

D **Alphabet Card Set** *grades 1–6*

E **Handwriting Positions Wall Chart**
   grades 1–6

F **Letter Cards** *grades K–2*

G **Story Journals** *grades K–4*

H **Keys to Legibility Wall Chart** *grades 2–6*

I **Alphabet Wall Strips** *grades 1–6*

J **Portfolio Assessment Guide** *grades 1–6*

For more information about these materials, call 1-800-421-3018.

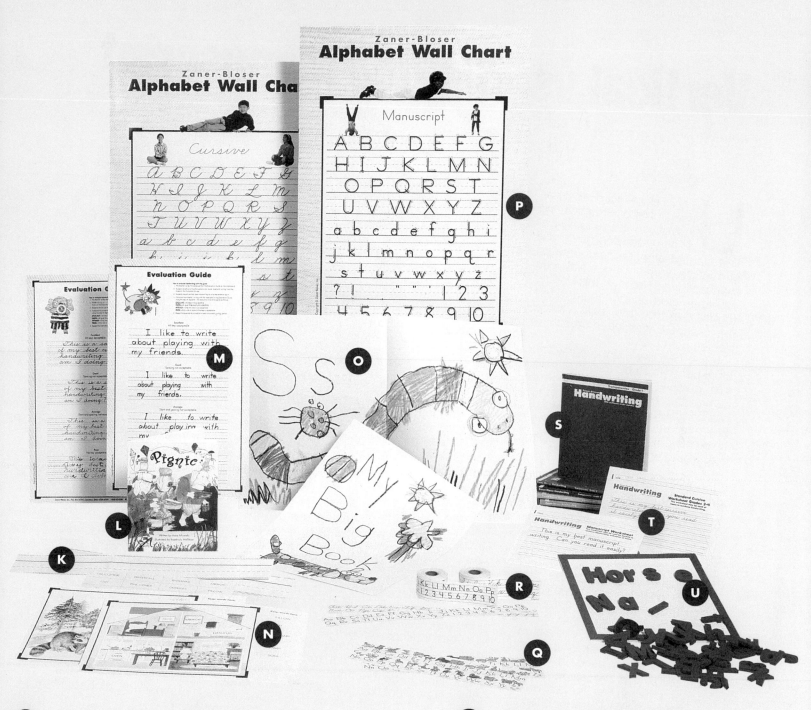

K **Blank Sentence Strips** *grades K–6*	**Q** **Illustrated Alphabet Strips** *grades K–2*
L **Pignic Alphabet Book** *grades K–2*	**R** **Desk Strips** *grades 1–6*
M **Evaluation Guides** *grades 1–6*	**S** **Book of Transparencies** *grades 1–6*
N **Vinyl Storyboard Set** *grades K–2*	**T** **Parent/Student Worksheets** *grades 2–6*
O **Make-Your-Own Big Book** *grades K–2*	**U** **Write-On, Wipe-Off Magnetic Board With Letters** *grades K–2*
P **Alphabet Wall Chart** *grades K–4*	

Vertical vs. *Slanted* Manuscript

What the research shows

Using a slanted alphabet has been a trend in handwriting instruction. It's actually not a new development—the first slanted alphabet was created in 1968. A sort of bridge between manuscript and cursive, this slanted alphabet used unconnected letterforms like the traditional vertical manuscript, but its letterforms were slanted like cursive.

It seemed like a good idea. This alphabet was to be easier to write than cursive, yet similar enough to cursive that children wouldn't learn two *completely* different alphabets. But after several years of use in some schools, research has uncovered some unfortunate findings.

Slanted manuscript can be difficult to write

Slanted manuscript was created to be similar to cursive, so it uses more complicated strokes such as small curves, and these strokes can be difficult for young children.

Vertical manuscript, on the other hand, is consistent with the development of young children. Each of its letters is formed with simple strokes—straight lines, circles, and slanted lines. One researcher found that the strokes used in vertical manuscript are the same as the shapes children use in their drawings (Farris, 1993). Because children are familiar with these shapes, they can identify and form the strokes with little difficulty.

Slanted manuscript can create problems with legibility

Legibility is an important goal in handwriting. Obviously, content should not be sacrificed for legibility, but what is handwriting if it cannot be read?

Educational researchers have tested the legibility of slanted manuscript and found that children writing vertical manuscript "performed significantly better" than those writing slanted manuscript. The writers of the slanted alphabet tended to make more misshapen letterforms, tended to extend their strokes above and below the guidelines, and had a difficult time keeping their letterforms consistent in size (Graham, 1992).

On the other hand, the vertical manuscript style of print has a lot of support in the area of research. Advertisers have known for years that italic type has a lower readability rate than vertical "roman" type. Research shows that in 30 minute readings, the italic style is read 4.9% slower than roman type (14–16 words per minute). This is why most literature, especially literature for early readers, is published using roman type.

Slanted manuscript can impair letter recognition

Educators have suspected that it would be beneficial for students to write and read the same style of alphabet. In other words, if children *read* vertical manuscript, they should also *write* vertical manuscript. Now it has been found that inconsistent alphabets may actually be detrimental to children's learning.

Researchers have found that slanted manuscript impairs the ability of some young children to recognize many letters. Some children who learn the slanted style alphabet find it difficult to recognize many of the traditional letterforms they see in books and environmental print. "[These children] consistently had difficulty identifying several letters, often making the same erroneous response to the same letter," the researchers reported. They concluded that slanted manuscript "creates substantially more letter recognition errors and causes more letter confusion than does the traditional style." (Kuhl & Dewitz, 1994).

Slanted manuscript does not help with transition

One of the benefits proposed by the creators of the slanted manuscript alphabet was that it made it easier for children to make the transition from manuscript to cursive writing. However, no difference in transition time has been found between the two styles of manuscript alphabets. In addition, the slanted style does not seem to enhance young children's production of cursive letters (Graham, 1992).

> *"...slanted manuscript letters cannot be recommended as a replacement for the traditional manuscript alphabet."*

The slanted style of manuscript appeared to be a good idea. But educators should take a close look at what the research shows before adopting this style of alphabet. As one researcher has said, "Given the lack of supportive evidence and the practical problems involved in implementation, slanted manuscript letters cannot be recommended as a replacement for the traditional manuscript alphabet" (Graham, 1994).

Farris, P.J. (1993). Learning to write the ABC's: A comparison of D'Nealian and Zaner-Bloser handwriting styles. *Indiana Reading Quarterly, 25* (4), 26–33.

Graham, S. (1992). Issues in handwriting instruction. *Focus on Exceptional Children, 25* (2).

Graham, S. (1994, Winter). Are slanted manuscript alphabets superior to the traditional manuscript alphabet? *Childhood Education,* 91–95.

Kuhl, D. & Dewitz, P. (1994, April). The effect of handwriting style on alphabet recognition. Paper presented at the annual meeting of the American Educational Research Association, New Orleans, LA.

Zaner-Bloser
Handwriting
With a new alphabet

Author
Clinton S. Hackney

Contributing Authors
Pamela J. Farris
Janice T. Jones
Linda Leonard Lamme

Zaner-Bloser, Inc.
P.O. Box 16764
Columbus, Ohio 43216-6764

Author

Clinton S. Hackney, Ed.D.

Contributing Authors

Pamela J. Farris, Ph.D.
Janice T. Jones, M.A.
Linda Leonard Lamme, Ph.D.

Reviewers

Judy L. Bausch, Grade 6, Columbus, Georgia
Cherlynn Bruce, Grade I, Conroe, Texas
Karen H. Burke, Director of Curriculum and Instruction,
    Bar Mills, Maine
Anne Chamberlin, Grade 2, Lynchburg, Virginia
Carol J. Fuhler, Grade 6, Flagstaff, Arizona
Deborah D. Gallagher, Grade 5, Gainesville, Florida
Kathleen Harrington, Grade 3, Redford, Michigan
Rebecca James, Grade 3, East Greenbush, New York
Gerald R. Maeckelbergh, Principal, Blaine, Minnesota
Bessie B. Peabody, Principal, East St. Louis, Illinois

Marilyn S. Petruska, Grade 5, Coraopolis, Pennsylvania
Sharon Ralph, Kindergarten, Nashville, Tennessee
Linda E. Ritchie, Grade 4, Birmingham, Alabama
Roberta Hogan Royer, Grade 2, North Canton, Ohio
Marion Redmond Starks, Grade 2, Baltimore, Maryland
Elizabeth J. Taglieri, Grade 2, Lake Zurich, Illinois
Claudia Williams, Grade 6, Lewisburg, West Virginia

Credits

Art: Marni Backer: 5, 62; Rosekrans Hoffman: 13, 18, 42, 51;
Claudia C. Kehrhahn: 60; Tom Leonard: 20, 22, 25, 45, 52;
Diane Paterson: 40; Sarah Snow: 24, 28, 30–31, 59, 61; Troy Viss:
19, 26, 41, 54, 56, 58; Andrea Wallace: 4, 27, 32, 34

Photos: John Lei/OPC: 6; Stephen Ogilvy: 8; Hubert
Manfred/Viesti Associates, *Dirt Road:* 38

Literature: "This Land Is Your Land." Words and Music by Woody
Guthrie. TRO© Copyright 1956 (Renewed), 1958 (Renewed) and
1970 Ludlow Music, Inc., New York, NY. Used by Permission.

Developed by Kirchoff/Wohlberg, Inc., in cooperation with Zaner-Bloser Publishers
Cover illustration by Lois Ehlert

ISBN 0-88085-710-2

Copyright © 1996 Zaner-Bloser, Inc.

CONTENTS

Did you know the word *cursive* comes from the Latin *currere*, which means "to run"? In this book, you'll "run" with cursive. After reviewing the strokes and letterforms, you'll improve your writing and pick up speed. You'll learn how to write quickly and legibly.

4

UNIT SUMMARY

This page tells students about the content, organization, and focus of the book. Students get started by taking a pretest to assess current ability. The lessons that follow review what students need to know to develop good handwriting skills.

PREVIEW THE BOOK

Preview the book with students, calling attention to its organization.

- Unit 1 presents handwriting basics.
- Unit 2 introduces lowercase and uppercase cursive letters grouped by common strokes.
- Unit 3 provides a variety of opportunities for students to write independently and to increase speed.

Point out that students will evaluate their handwriting frequently. Set up a portfolio for each student to assess individual progress throughout the year.

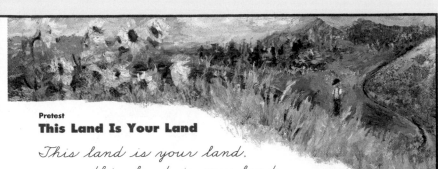

Pretest

This Land Is Your Land

This land is your land.
this land is my land
From California to the New York island.
From the redwood forest to the
Gulf Stream waters
This land was made for you and me.

As I was walking that ribbon of highway.
I saw above me that endless skyway.
I saw below me that golden valley
This land was made for you and me.

Woody Guthrie

On your paper, write the first stanza of this American folk song in your best cursive writing.

EVALUATE	Are all your tall letters the same size?	Yes	No
	Are your short letters half the height of your tall letters?	Yes	No
	Did you avoid collisions?	Yes	No
	Does your writing have uniform slant?	Yes	No
	Is your spacing correct?	Yes	No

5

EVALUATE

As students write, monitor and informally assess their performance. Then guide them through the self-evaluation process. Meet individually with students to help them assess their handwriting. Ask them how they would like to improve their writing. (visual, auditory)

PRETEST

Have students use the first stanza of the folk song as a model for writing. Remind them to use correct letter size and shape, uniform slant, and correct spacing as they write. Tell students to place their pretests in their writing portfolios so they can write the same selection for the posttest later in the year. (visual, auditory, kinesthetic)

COACHING HINT: SELF-EVALUATION

Self-evaluation is an important step in the handwriting process. By identifying their own strengths and weaknesses, students become independent learners.

The steps in the self-evaluation process are as follows:

1. Question
Students should ask themselves questions such as these: "Is my slant correct?" "Do my letters rest on the baseline?"

2. Compare
Students should compare their handwriting to correct models.

3. Evaluate
Students should determine strengths and weaknesses in their handwriting based on the keys to legibility.

4. Diagnose
Students should diagnose the cause of any difficulties. Possible causes include incorrect paper or pencil position, inconsistent pressure on pencil, and incorrect strokes.

5. Improve
Self-evaluation should include a means of improvement through additional instruction and continued practice. (visual, auditory, kinesthetic)

WRITING POSITIONS

Suggest that students refer to this page throughout the year as a reminder of proper posture and correct paper and pencil position. Demonstrate correct positions for both left-handed and right-handed writers. Then ask students to place a sheet of paper in the proper position on their desks, pick up a pencil, and write their names. (visual, auditory, kinesthetic)

COACHING HINT

You may wish to group left-handed students together for instruction if you can do so without calling attention to the practice. They should be seated to the left of the chalkboard.

Writing Positions

If you are left-handed . . .

Sit up and hold your pencil this way. Slant your paper with the lower right corner pointing toward you.

If you are right-handed . . .

Sit up and hold your pencil this way. Slant your paper with the lower left corner pointing toward you.

6

PENCIL POSITION

left hand

right hand

PAPER POSITION

left hand

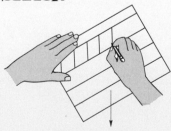

right hand

EVALUATE

Check for correct paper and pencil positions. The Zaner-Bloser Writing Frame can be used to improve hand position. (visual, kinesthetic)

Cursive Letters and Numerals

Aa Bb Cc Dd Ee Ff Gg
Hh Ii Jj Kk Ll Mm
Nn Oo Pp Qq Rr Ss Tt
Uu Vv Ww Xx Yy Zz
1 2 3 4 5 6 7 8 9 10

Write your initials, your nickname, and your full name.
_____
_____

Write your birth date and your age.
_____

Write the title of your favorite book or song.
_____
_____

Write the letters and numerals you want to improve.
_____
_____

7

EVALUATE
Poll students to find out which letters and numerals are most difficult for them to write. Discuss the problems students identify. (auditory)

CURSIVE LETTERS AND NUMERALS
Students can use the chart at the top of the page to review cursive letters and numerals. (visual, auditory)

COACHING HINT
Review with students the use of guidelines for correct letter formation. Draw guidelines on the chalkboard, and invite volunteers to write words on the guidelines. (visual, auditory, kinesthetic)

COACHING HINT: USE OF THE CHALKBOARD
You and your students can follow these suggestions for writing on the chalkboard.

Left-Hander. Stand in front of the writing lines and pull the downstrokes to the left elbow. The elbow is bent, and the writing is done at a comfortable height. Step to the right often to maintain correct slant.

Right-Hander. Stand to the left of the writing lines and pull the downstrokes toward the midsection of the body. The elbow is bent, and the writing is done at a comfortable height. Step to the right often to maintain correct slant. (visual, kinesthetic)

IMPORTANT STROKES FOR CURSIVE WRITING

UNDERCURVE
Curve under and up.

UNDERCURVE
Curve under and up.

DOWNCURVE
Curve left and down.

DOWNCURVE
Curve left and down.

OVERCURVE
Curve up and right.

OVERCURVE
Curve up and right.

SLANT
Slant left.

SLANT
Slant left.

Important Strokes for Cursive Writing

Undercurve   Downcurve   Overcurve   Slant

Undercurves swing.   Undercurve, downcurve,
Downcurves dive.   Overcurve, slant.
Overcurves bounce.   As you write cursive letters,
Slants just slide.   Remember this chant.

Write these letters.   Circle the strokes you use.

e e e

u u u

d d d

m m m

a a a

n n n

8

MODEL THE WRITING

Model the two sizes of each stroke on guidelines. Invite students to say the names as they write the strokes in the air. Point out that cursive letters are formed from these basic strokes. Suggest that students name the strokes as they write each letter to complete the page. (visual, auditory, kinesthetic)

Keys to Legibility

To help make your writing legible, pay attention to size and shape, slant, and spacing.

Size and Shape

Tall letters should not touch the headline.

Some lowercase letters are tall letters.

All uppercase letters are tall letters.

Numerals are the same height as tall letters.

b   f   t
A   B   C
1   2   3

Short letters should be half the height of tall letters.

Some lowercase letters are short letters.

a   g   n

Descenders should not go too far below the baseline.

Some lowercase letters have descenders.

Some uppercase letters have descenders.

f   g   j
J   Y   Z

Write the words beneath the models. Pay careful attention to the size and shape of your letters.

legible   cursive   writing

communicate   penmanship

EVALUATE Compare your words with the models.
Are your letters the correct size and shape?   Yes   No

9

MODEL THE WRITING

Model writing a tall letter, a short letter, and a letter with a descender, noting the placement of each letter on the guidelines. Remind students that all letters of the same size should be the same height. (visual, auditory)

EVALUATE

Guide students through the self-evaluation process. Then ask if they can read their words easily. Encourage them to explain why or why not. (visual, auditory)

UNIT SUMMARY

This lesson serves as an introduction to Unit 2. The lessons that follow emphasize cursive letter formation and joinings. The Teacher Edition includes information on optional joinings of uppercase letters. Evaluations focus on letter size and shape.

PREVIEW THE UNIT

Preview the unit with students, calling attention to these features:

* letter models with numbered directional arrows
* guidelines for student writing directly beneath handwriting models
* reminders about joining letters
* geographical facts
* independent writing activities
* opportunities to evaluate letter size and shape

COACHING HINT

Demonstrate for students the technique of drawing a horizontal line with a ruler along the tops of their letters to show proper size. Have them practice this technique periodically to evaluate their letter size in curriculum areas that require handwriting, especially those that involve writing sentences or paragraphs. (visual, auditory, kinesthetic)

Slant

The slant of your writing should be uniform.

All your letters should slant forward.

dd b b d b

Check the slant. Draw lines through the slant strokes of the letters.

Are your lines parallel?

Spacing

Your spacing should be correct.

between letters   *letters*

between words   *word word*

between sentences   *end. O Begin*

Check the spacing. Write *O* between letters, \ between words, and *O* between sentences.

Make sure your spacing is correct. Shift your paper as you write.

Write this sentence. Pay careful attention to slant and spacing.

This is my best handwriting.

EVALUATE   Does your writing have uniform slant?   Yes   No
Is your spacing correct?   Yes   No

10

MODEL THE WRITING

To show an example of correct slant and spacing, write the following sentences on guidelines: *My writing is legible. The slant and the spacing are correct.* Invite students to check the slant by drawing lines through the slant strokes in the letters and to check the spacing by drawing ovals between letters, by drawing slanted lines between words, and by writing uppercase **O** between sentences. (visual, auditory, kinesthetic)

EVALUATE

Guide students through the self-evaluation process. Then ask them if they can read their sentences easily. Encourage them to explain why or why not. (visual, auditory)

Write Undercurve Letters

Write the letters, joinings, and words.

i   *i*   *i*   *i*   *ir*   *id*   *im*

irregular   *idle*   *important*

t   *t*   *t*   *t*   *tr*   *to*   *ty*

traveler   *topic*   *type*

u   *u*   *u*   *u*   *us*   *ud*   *un*

usually   *student*   *understand*

CHECKSTROKE ALERT

w   *w*   *w*   *w*   *wh*   *wo*   *wy*

wherever   *wolves*   *snowy*

EVALUATE Circle your best joining.
Circle your best word.

11

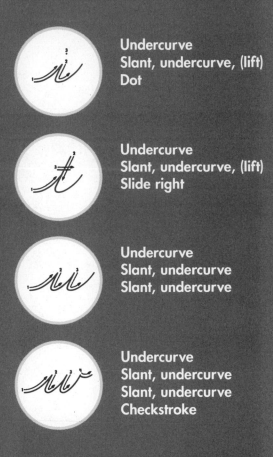

Undercurve
Slant, undercurve, (lift)
Dot

Undercurve
Slant, undercurve, (lift)
Slide right

Undercurve
Slant, undercurve
Slant, undercurve

Undercurve
Slant, undercurve
Slant, undercurve
Checkstroke

MODEL THE WRITING

Model each letter and say the stroke descriptions, emphasizing the beginning undercurve stroke in each. Ask questions such as these:
In what ways are the letters alike?
Which letter ends with a checkstroke?
Which letters have a lift?
How is **w** different from **u**?
(visual, auditory)

EVALUATE

To help students evaluate their writing, ask questions such as these:
Did you pull the slant strokes to the baseline?
Are the slant strokes in **u** and **w** parallel?
Do all your letters rest on the baseline?
(visual, auditory)

Name

Write the letters, joinings, and words.

i   *i*   *i*   *is*   *ig*   *in*

misjudge delight instant

t   *t*   *t*   *th*   *ta*   *tm*

through tax appointment

u   *u*   *u*   *ur*   *ua*   *um*

urban guard umbrella

CHECKSTROKE ALERT

w   *w*   *w*   *we*   *wa*   *wn*

weather waste blown

EVALUATE Circle your best joining.
Circle your best word.

Copyright © Zaner-Bloser, Inc.   **PRACTICE MASTER I**

PRACTICE MASTER I

Undercurve
Slant right
Slant, undercurve

Undercurve
Retrace, curve down
   and back
Undercurve

Undercurve
Slant, loop back
Overcurve, curve back
Undercurve

Undercurve
Slant
Loop back, overcurve,
   (lift)
Dot

Write Undercurve Letters

Write the letters, joinings, and words.

r   r   r   re   ro   rn

receive   robot   modern

s   s   s   se   sc   sm

seize   science   nonsmoking

p   p   p   pl   pa   pm

pleasant   patient   chipmunk

j   j   j   ju   ja   jo

judgment   jacket   joyous

EVALUATE Circle your best joining.
Circle your best word.

12

Practice Master (insert)

Name

Write the letters, joinings, and words.

r   r   r   ru   ra   ry

ruler   ratio   secondary

s   s   s   sh   sa   sy

shampoo   satellite   system

p   p   p   pr   po   py

prison   position   pyramid

j   j   j   je   ju   ja

jewelry   jingle   janitor

EVALUATE Circle your best joining.
Circle your best word.

Copyright © Zaner-Bloser, Inc.   **PRACTICE MASTER 2**

PRACTICE MASTER 2

MODEL THE WRITING

Model each letter and say the stroke descriptions, emphasizing the beginning undercurve stroke in each. Ask questions such as these:
How do all the letters begin?
Which letters have descenders?
Which letter ends with an overcurve?
How do the other letters end?
(visual, auditory)

EVALUATE

To help students evaluate their writing, ask questions such as these:
Does your **r** have correct slant?
Do the loops of your **p** and **j** close at the baseline?
(visual, auditory)

Review

Sort the words. Write each one in the correct category.
Use a dictionary to check word meanings.

ultrasaurus   *ibis*   *shallot*   *lentil*
rutabaga   *parsnip*   *jicama*   *rhea*
watermelon   *rhubarb*   *jaguar*   *sloth*
terrapin   *platypus*   *taro*   *wombat*

Animal	Vegetable
ultrasaurus	rutabaga
terrapin	watermelon
ibis	parsnip
platypus	rhubarb
jaguar	shallot
rhea	jicama
sloth	taro
wombat	lentil

On Your Own Add four words of your own to the chart.

EVALUATE Did you join your letters correctly?   Yes   No
Did you close each *s*, *p*, and *j*?   Yes   No

13

EVALUATE

Guide students through the self-evaluation process, focusing on letter formation and joinings. Encourage students to explain why one letter or joining they wrote might be better than another. (visual, auditory)

REFOCUS

Write the undercurve letters **i, t, u, w, r, s, p,** and **j** as you say the stroke descriptions. Review the undercurve to undercurve, overcurve to undercurve, and checkstroke to undercurve joinings (**it, ju, wr**).

Pair students and give them a two-minute period to write quickly but legibly as many words as possible containing **it, ju,** and **wr**. Ask volunteers to write their lists of words on the chalkboard, paying close attention to forming and joining the letters correctly. (visual, auditory, kinesthetic)

COACHING HINT

Keep a record of the letters students are having problems with. Provide practice with these letters by assigning writing exercises such as making word lists and writing tongue twisters. (visual, auditory, kinesthetic)

WRITE AWAY

Ask students to make their own classification worksheets. Suggest they add *Mineral* to the categories *Animal* and *Vegetable* or use different categories, such as *People, Places,* and *Things.*

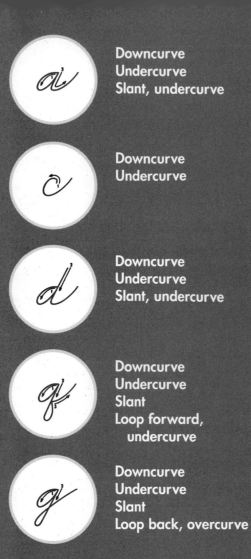

a
Downcurve
Undercurve
Slant, undercurve

c
Downcurve
Undercurve

d
Downcurve
Undercurve
Slant, undercurve

q
Downcurve
Undercurve
Slant
Loop forward,
  undercurve

g
Downcurve
Undercurve
Slant
Loop back, overcurve

o
Downcurve
Undercurve
Checkstroke

Name

Write the letters, joinings, and words.

a a a   c c c
ar ag ay   cl ca cm
arrive   capital
d d d   q q q
de do dn   qu qu qu
desire   quart
g g g   **CHECKSTROKE ALERT**
gr go gy   o o o
governor   ou oa ox
           oxygen

EVALUATE Circle your best joining.
Circle your best word.

Copyright © Zaner-Bloser, Inc.   **PRACTICE MASTER 3**

PRACTICE MASTER 3

14

Write Downcurve Letters

Write the letters, joinings, and words.

a
a a a
al ac ax
aloud

c
c c c
ce co cy
bicycle

d
d d d
di da dy
daisies

q
q q q
qu qu qu
quotient

g
g g g
ge ga gn
geometry

CHECKSTROKE ALERT
o
o o o
of oc ov
ocean

EVALUATE Circle your best joining.
Circle your best word.

14

MODEL THE WRITING

Model each letter and say the stroke descriptions, emphasizing the downcurve stroke in each. Ask questions such as these:
How are **a** and **d** alike?
How does **g** differ from **q**?
How are **o** and **c** alike?
How does **o** end?
(visual, auditory)

EVALUATE

To help students evaluate their writing, ask questions such as these:
Do all your letters have correct slant?
Did you pull the slant strokes in **a** and **d** to the baseline?
Do the loops of your **q** and **g** close at the baseline?
(visual, auditory)

Write Overcurve Letters

Write the letters, joinings, and words.

m   m   m   m

m   m   m   m

nt   ng   nn   mi   ma   mm

prevent   midair

x   x   x   x   y   y   y   y

xp   xa   xy   ye   yo   yn

explained   lawyer

z   z   z   z

CHECKSTROKE ALERT

v   v   v   v

ze   zo   zz   vi   va   vy

ozone   heavy

EVALUATE Circle your best joining.
Circle your best word.

15

MODEL THE WRITING

Model each letter and say the stroke descriptions, emphasizing the beginning overcurve stroke in each. Ask questions such as these:

How do all the letters begin?

Which letters end with an overcurve?

Which letter has a lift?

(visual, auditory)

EVALUATE

To help students evaluate their writing, ask questions such as these:

Is your **x** crossed in the middle of the slant stroke?

Does your **v** end with a checkstroke?

Is each letter about the same width as the model?

(visual, auditory)

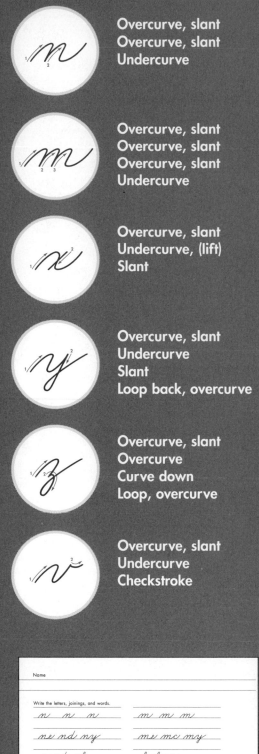

m
Overcurve, slant
Overcurve, slant
Undercurve

m
Overcurve, slant
Overcurve, slant
Overcurve, slant
Undercurve

x
Overcurve, slant
Undercurve, (lift)
Slant

y
Overcurve, slant
Undercurve
Slant
Loop back, overcurve

z
Overcurve, slant
Overcurve
Curve down
Loop, overcurve

v
Overcurve, slant
Undercurve
Checkstroke

Name

Write the letters, joinings, and words.

m   m   m   m   m   m

ne   nd   ny   me   mc   my

neutral   balmy

x   x   x   y   y   y

xe   xc   xn   yi   ya   ym

excite   yield

z   z   z   **CHECKSTROKE ALERT**

zi   za   zy   v   v   v

zigzag   ve   vo   vy

            volt

EVALUATE Circle your best joining.
Circle your best word.

PRACTICE MASTER 4

PRACTICE MASTER 4

Refer students to the cursive alphabet on page 7. Ask them to locate the six lowercase letters that begin with a downcurve (**a**, **c**, **d**, **q**, **g**, **o**) and the six lowercase letters that begin with an overcurve (**n**, **m**, **x**, **y**, **z**, **v**). Invite volunteers to write each letter on the chalkboard and name the ending stroke.

Have students write various combinations of three of the twelve letters on the chalkboard as they identify the joining strokes. Students can use colored chalk to highlight the joinings. (visual, auditory, kinesthetic)

COACHING HINT

Remind students that a little more space is needed before words that begin with a downcurve letter (**a**, **c**, **d**, **q**, **g**, **o**). Write a sentence on the chalkboard, for example, *An alligator gave the ducks quite a scare*. Use colored chalk to indicate where more space is needed. (visual, auditory)

WRITE AWAY

Ask students to write sentences using three related compound words from page 16. Participate by sharing sentences with students.

Review

air   cat   day   extra   golden   moon
night   out   quick   video   yard   zero

Choose and write a word that goes with each set of words.
Use a dictionary if you need help.

break	dream	time	*day*
club	fall	gown	night
line	mail	port	air
sand	silver	step	quick
field	fit	law	out
rod	rule	wedding	golden
cassette	phone	tape	video
beam	light	walk	moon
ordinary	sensory	terrestrial	extra
bird	call	tail	cat
hour	gravity	in on	zero
line	sale	stick	yard

On Your Own Write three words that go with the word *down*.

EVALUATE Did you join your letters correctly?   Yes   No
Do your letters have uniform slant?   Yes   No

16

EVALUATE

Guide students through the self-evaluation process, focusing on letter slant and joinings. Encourage students to explain why one letter or joining they wrote might be better than another. (visual, auditory)

Write Letters With Loops

Write the letters, joinings, and words.

e | e e e
l | l l l
ei ec em | ls lo ly
eighty | lying

h | h h h
k | k k k
ht ha hy | ki ko kn
handsome | kilometer

f | f f f
fr fo fy | **CHECKSTROKE ALERT**
frontier | *b* | b b b
| bi ba by
| bifocals

EVALUATE Circle your best joining.
Circle your best word.

17

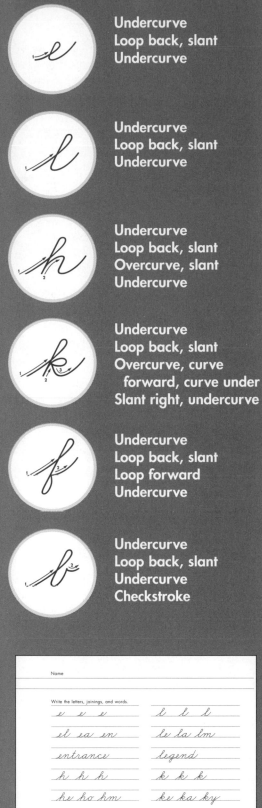

Undercurve
Loop back, slant
Undercurve

Undercurve
Loop back, slant
Undercurve

Undercurve
Loop back, slant
Overcurve, slant
Undercurve

Undercurve
Loop back, slant
Overcurve, curve
   forward, curve under
Slant right, undercurve

Undercurve
Loop back, slant
Loop forward
Undercurve

Undercurve
Loop back, slant
Undercurve
Checkstroke

MODEL THE WRITING

Model each letter and say the stroke descriptions, emphasizing the beginning loop in each. Ask questions such as these:
In what ways are the letters alike?
Which letters end with an undercurve?
How does **b** end?
(visual, auditory)

EVALUATE

To help students evaluate their writing, ask questions such as these:
Are all your letters the correct size?
Is the forward curve of your **k** closed?
Does the lower loop of your **f** close at the baseline?
(visual, auditory)

Name _____

Write the letters, joinings, and words.

e e e | l l l
el ea en | le la lm
entrance | legend
h h h | k k k
he ho hm | ke ka ky
hobbies | karate
f f f | **CHECKSTROKE ALERT**
fl fa fy | b b b
fluoride | bu bo by
| nearby

EVALUATE Circle your best joining.
Circle your best word.

Copyright © Zaner-Bloser, Inc.

PRACTICE MASTER 5

PRACTICE MASTER 5

17

REFOCUS
Write the six letters with loops (**e, l, h, k, f, b**). Ask students to think of words spelled with one or more of these letters. Write their responses, incorrectly closing the loops in some of the letters.

Ask students to locate, describe, and correct the errors. Have students name the strokes as they form the letters with loops. (visual, auditory, kinesthetic)

COACHING HINT
Students' progress in handwriting is greater when short, intensive periods of instruction are used. Fifteen minutes for a lesson is optimal.

WRITE AWAY
Challenge students to write riddles for homophone pairs. Participate by providing an example, such as *What do you call the main rule of conduct? (the principal principle)*

Review

beagle	billy	bog	deer
fake	frog	glen	goose
hawk	hen	legal	loose
silly	snake	spear	talk

Choose and write a pair of rhyming words to answer each question.

What is a foolish male goat?

What is a valley for female fowls?

What is conversation among birds of prey?

What is a runaway bird?

What is a home for amphibians?

What is a synthetic boa?

What is a dog with a license?

What is a buck's antler?

silly billy

hen	glen
hawk	talk
loose	goose
frog	bog
fake	snake
legal	beagle
deer	spear

On Your Own Write a question about a pair of rhyming words. Ask a friend to answer it.

EVALUATE Are the loops in each e, l, h, k, f, and b open?   Yes   No

18

EVALUATE
Guide students through the self-evaluation process, focusing on letter formation. Encourage students to explain why one letter they wrote might be better than another. (visual, auditory)

Manuscript Maintenance

The Hawaiian alphabet has only these twelve letters.

| a | e | i | o | u | h | k | l | m | n | p | w |

Use these letters to form as many words as you can. Write in lowercase manuscript.

EVALUATE Are your letters formed correctly? Yes No

DID YOU KNOW? The Hawaiian alphabet also has a symbol ʻ called "Okina."

EVALUATE

Have students focus on size and shape to determine whether their lowercase manuscript letters are legible. Discuss ways to improve legibility. (visual, auditory)

BEFORE WRITING

On the chalkboard, write this sentence in manuscript: *E'olelo Hawai'i wale no ma 'ane'i.* (Only Hawaiian spoken here.) Point out that Hawaii is the only state that has two official languages: English and Hawaiian.

MANUSCRIPT MAINTENANCE

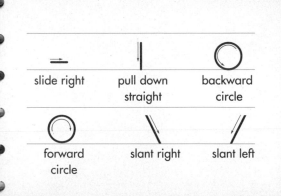

| slide right | pull down straight | backward circle |
| forward circle | slant right | slant left |

Review the basic strokes for manuscript writing. Remind students that all manuscript letters are formed with these strokes and that manuscript writing is vertical. Have students practice the strokes and letterforms. Tell them to adjust the position of the paper for manuscript writing. (visual, auditory, kinesthetic)

WRITE AWAY

Ask students to use the first thirteen letters of the alphabet to write as many words as they can. Have students write in lowercase manuscript.

COACHING HINT

To reinforce manuscript writing, have students use manuscript to prepare invitations to parties, to send holiday greetings, and to label maps and diagrams.

Downcurve
Undercurve
Slant, undercurve

Slant
Downcurve
Undercurve

Slant
Downcurve, loop
Downcurve,
**   undercurve**

Downcurve
Undercurve
Loop, curve right

Write Downcurve Letters

a, C, and E are joined to the letter that follows.
O is not joined to the letter that follows.

Write the letters, joinings, and words. Then write the sentence.

a   a   a   Al   Ac   An

Alaska   Acapulco   Anchorage

C   C   Cl   Ca   Cy

Cleveland   Canada   Cyprus

E   E   El   Ec   En

El Paso   Ecuador   England

O   O   Ohio   Omaha

DID YOU KNOW?

Ohio has a state drink.

EVALUATE Circle your best word.

20

MODEL THE WRITING

Model each letter and say the stroke descriptions, emphasizing the downcurve stroke in each. Ask questions such as these:
Which letters begin with a downcurve?
Which letters begin with slant, downcurve?
Where is the loop in **O**?
(visual, auditory)

EVALUATE

To help students evaluate their writing, ask questions such as these:
Are all your letters the correct size?
Do your letters have correct slant?
Did you close your **A** and your **O**?
(visual, auditory)

Name

a, C, and E are joined to the letter that follows.
O is not joined to the letter that follows.

Write the letters, joinings, and words. Then write the sentence.

a a a Au Ad Am

Australia Aden America

C C C Ch Co Cy

Chicago Colombia Cyrene

E E E Eu Ed Ev

Europe Edinburgh Everglades

O O O Oregon Oxford

DID YOU KNOW?

Oxford is in England.

EVALUATE Circle your best word.

    PRACTICE MASTER 6

PRACTICE MASTER 6

Write Curve Forward Letters

n, m, K, and *H* are joined to the letter that follows.

Write the letters, joinings, and words.

n   n   n   Ni   No   Ny

Nigeria   Norway   Nyack

m   m   m   Me   Ma   My

Mexico   Maine   Myrtle Beach

K   K   K   Ki   Ka   Kn

Kiev   Kansas   Knoxville

H   H   H   He   Ho   Hy

Helsinki   Honolulu   Hyannis

EVALUATE Circle your best word.

21

Curve forward, slant
Overcurve, slant
Undercurve

Curve forward, slant
Overcurve, slant
Overcurve, slant
Undercurve

Curve forward, slant,
  (lift)
Doublecurve
Curve forward,
  undercurve

Curve forward, slant,
  (lift)
Curve back, slant
Retrace, loop, curve
  right

MODEL THE WRITING

Model each letter and say the stroke descriptions, emphasizing the curve forward, slant strokes in each. Ask questions such as these:
How are **H** and **K** alike?
How does **N** differ from **M**?
How many slant strokes does each letter have?
(visual, auditory)

EVALUATE

To help students evaluate their writing, ask questions such as these:
Are your slant strokes parallel?
Is each letter about the same width as the model?
Is the second overcurve in your **M** shorter than the first?
(visual, auditory)

Name

n, m, K, and *H* are joined to the letter that follows.

Write the letters, joinings, and words.

n   n   n   Ne   Na   No

Nevada   Naples   Nova Scotia

m   m   m   Mi   Mo   Ma

Michigan   Morocco   Malaysia

K   K   K   Ke   Ko   Ky

Kentucky   Korea   Kyoto

H   H   H   He   Ha   Hy

Helena   Haiti   Hyde Park

EVALUATE Circle your best word.

PRACTICE MASTER 7

PRACTICE MASTER 7

REFOCUS

On the chalkboard write the downcurve letters **A, C, E,** and **O** and the curve forward letters **N, M, K,** and **H.** Then have students write each letter twice. Ask these questions:

Which letters are joined to the letter that follows?

Which letter is not joined to the letter that follows?

Have students pay attention to upper-case letter formation and joinings as they write the names of

• a continent beginning with **A**

• a city beginning with **C**

• a boy beginning with **E**

• a state beginning with **O**

• a planet beginning with **N**

• a country beginning with **M**

• a girl beginning with **K**

• a family beginning with **H**

(visual, auditory, kinesthetic)

COACHING HINT

Holding the pencil too tightly is a common problem that causes students to tire easily when writing. To help students overcome this problem, have them crumple a piece of paper, place it in the palm of the writing hand, and pick up the pencil. This will serve as a reminder not to squeeze the pencil. (kinesthetic)

WRITE AWAY

Have students choose one of the events listed on page 22, imagine what it might be like, and write a paragraph describing it. Participate by sharing your ideas.

22

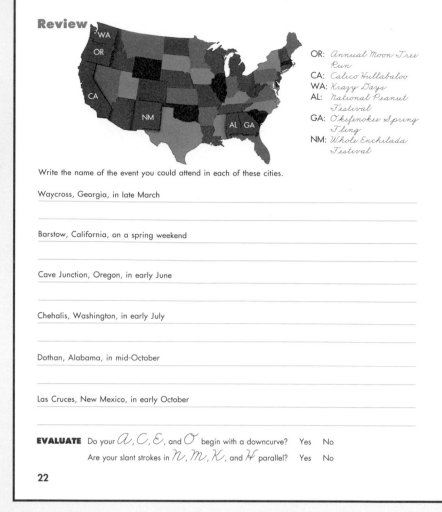

Review

OR: Annual Moon Tree Run
CA: Calico Hullabaloo
WA: Krazy Days
AL: National Peanut Festival
GA: Okefenokee Spring Fling
NM: Whole Enchilada Festival

Write the name of the event you could attend in each of these cities.

Waycross, Georgia, in late March

Barstow, California, on a spring weekend

Cave Junction, Oregon, in early June

Chehalis, Washington, in early July

Dothan, Alabama, in mid-October

Las Cruces, New Mexico, in early October

EVALUATE Do your *a, C, E,* and *O* begin with a downcurve?   Yes   No

Are your slant strokes in *N, M, K,* and *H* parallel?   Yes   No

22

EVALUATE

Guide students through the self-evaluation process, focusing on letter formation and slant. Encourage students to explain why one letter they wrote might be better than another. (visual, auditory)

Write Curve Forward Letters

U, Y, and *Z* are joined to the letter that follows.
V, X, and *W* are not joined to the letter that follows.

Write the letters, joinings, and words.

U   *U*   *U*   *Ut*   *Ug*   *Un*

Utah   *Uganda*   *Union City*

Y   *Y*   *Yu*   *Ya*   *Yo*

Yuma   *Yakima*   *Yonkers*

Z   *Z*   *Zu*   *Za*   *Zo*

Zurich   *Zanesville*   *Zomba*

V   *V*   *Vermont*   *Vallejo*

X   *X*   *Xiamen*   *Xuanhua*

W   *W*   *Wisconsin*   *Wyoming*

EVALUATE Circle your best word.

23

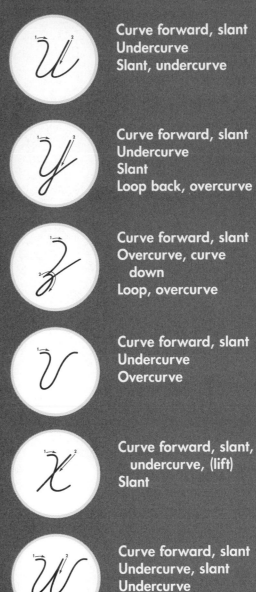

Curve forward, slant
Undercurve
Slant, undercurve

Curve forward, slant
Undercurve
Slant
Loop back, overcurve

Curve forward, slant
Overcurve, curve
  down
Loop, overcurve

Curve forward, slant
Undercurve
Overcurve

Curve forward, slant,
  undercurve, (lift)
Slant

Curve forward, slant
Undercurve, slant
Undercurve
Overcurve

MODEL THE WRITING

Model each letter and say the stroke descriptions, emphasizing the curve forward, slant strokes in each. Ask questions such as these:
How do all the letters begin?
Which letters end with an overcurve?
Which letter has a lift?
(visual, auditory)

EVALUATE

To help students evaluate their writing, ask questions such as these:
Did you pull the slant strokes in **U** to the baseline?
Do the loops of your **Y** and **Z** close at the baseline?
Is each letter about the same width as the model?
(visual, auditory)

Joining Alert

Joining **X** to the letter that follows is optional.

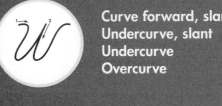

PRACTICE MASTER 8

23

Slant, curve forward
    and right, (lift)
Doublecurve, curve up
Retrace, curve right

Slant, curve forward
    and right, (lift)
Doublecurve, curve up
Retrace, curve right,
    (lift)
Slide right

Overcurve
Curve down and up
Retrace, curve right

Curve back, overcurve
Curve down, retrace
Curve forward, curve
    under

Overcurve
Slant
Loop back, overcurve

Write Doublecurve and Overcurve Letters

$\mathcal{T}$, $\mathcal{F}$, $\mathcal{I}$, and $\mathcal{Q}$ are not joined to the letter that follows.
$\mathcal{J}$ is joined to the letter that follows.

Write the letters, joinings, and words. Then write the sentences.

$\mathcal{T}$ $\mathcal{T}$ $\mathcal{T}$ Texas   Tyler

$\mathcal{F}$ $\mathcal{F}$ $\mathcal{F}$ Florida   Fort Lee

$\mathcal{I}$ $\mathcal{I}$ $\mathcal{I}$ Iowa   Independence

$\mathcal{Q}$ $\mathcal{Q}$ Queensland   Quincy

$\mathcal{J}$ $\mathcal{J}$ Ju   Ja   Jo

Juneau   Jamaica   Joplin

DID YOU KNOW?

Texas chose the first state tree.

The oak is Iowa's state tree.

EVALUATE Circle your best word.

24

PRACTICE MASTER 9

24

MODEL THE WRITING

Model each letter and say the stroke descriptions, emphasizing the doublecurve in **T** and **F** and the overcurve in **I, J,** and **Q**. Ask students questions such as these:
Which letters have a doublecurve?
Which letters have an overcurve?
Which letters have a lift?
(visual, auditory)

EVALUATE

To help students evaluate their writing, ask questions such as these:
Does your **F** have a slide right stroke?
Do the loops of your **J** close at the baseline?
Does your **Q** end below the baseline?
(visual, auditory)

Joining Alert
Joining **T, F,** and **I** to the letter that follows is optional.

Review

Fort Wayne Philharmonic   *Opera San Jose*
Orchestra of Santa Fe   *Utah Symphony*
Orchestre Symphonique de Quebec   *Tulsa Ballet Theatre*
Rhode Island Philharmonic   *Virginia Opera*
Youngstown Symphony

Write where you can go to the symphony, opera, or ballet in each of these cities.

San Jose, California

Fort Wayne, Indiana

Santa Fe, New Mexico

Youngstown, Ohio

Tulsa, Oklahoma

Providence, Rhode Island

Salt Lake City, Utah

Norfolk, Virginia

Quebec, Canada

EVALUATE   Are your uppercase letters formed correctly?   Yes   No
Do your letters rest on the baseline?   Yes   No

25

EVALUATE

Guide students through the self-evaluation process, focusing on letter formation and slant. Encourage students to explain why one letter they wrote might be better than another. (visual, auditory)

REFOCUS

Refer students to the cursive alphabet on page 7. Ask them to locate these six uppercase letters that begin with curve forward, slant strokes: **U, Y, Z, V, X, W**. Repeat for doublecurve letters **T** and **F** and overcurve letters **I, J,** and **Q**.
Ask these questions:
Which letters are joined to the letter that follows?
Which letters are not joined to the letter that follows?

Ask volunteers to write the letters on the chalkboard, and have students suggest words that begin with the letters. Write each word, saying the stroke descriptions for the initial uppercase letter. Highlight the stroke that names each letter grouping. (visual, auditory, kinesthetic)

COACHING HINT

Give each student a card on which one of the basic strokes is written. Tell students to write that basic stroke and then to write all the uppercase and lowercase letters that have that stroke. If time permits, have students trade cards and do the same with a different basic stroke. (visual, kinesthetic)

WRITE AWAY

Ask students to write a list of ono-matopoeic words to describe sounds at the ballet, symphony, or opera. Provide examples, such as the boom of a kettle-drum, the plink of a piano, or the mur-mur of the audience.

Undercurve, loop,
curve forward
Doublecurve, curve up
Retrace, curve right

Undercurve, loop
Curve down and up
Retrace, curve right

Undercurve
Loop, curve down
Loop, curve under

Doublecurve
Loop, curve down
and up
Loop, curve right

Write Letters With Loops

G, S, L, and *D* are not joined to the letter that follows.

Write the letters and words. Then write the sentences.

G   G   G   Georgia   Galveston

S   S   S   Salem   South Dakota

L   L   L   Louisiana   Lynchburg

D   D   D   Delaware   Daytona

DID YOU KNOW?

Georgia has a state atlas.

South Dakota has a state fish.

Louisiana has a state reptile.

Delaware has a state bug.

EVALUATE Circle your best word.

26

26

MODEL THE WRITING

Model each letter and say the stroke descriptions, emphasizing the initial loop in each. Ask questions such as these:
Which letters begin at the baseline?
Which letters have a loop that rests on the baseline?
Which letter ends below the baseline?
(visual, auditory)

EVALUATE

To help students evaluate their writing, ask questions such as these:
Do all your letters have correct slant?
Is each letter about the same width as the model?
Does your **D** touch the baseline twice?
(visual, auditory)

Joining Alert
Joining **G** and **S** to the letter that follows is optional.

Write Undercurve-Slant Letters

P and *B* are not joined to the letter that follows.
R is joined to the letter that follows.

Write the letters, joinings, and words. Then write the sentences.

P   *P*   *P*   *Plymouth*   *Point Barrow*

B   *B*   *Beloit*   *Boston*

R   *R*   *Rh*   *Ro*   *Ry*

Rhode Island   *Rockford*   *Rye*

DID YOU KNOW?

Plymouth Rock is famous.

A Boston terrier is a dog.

A Rhode Island Red is a bird.

EVALUATE Circle your best word.

27

Undercurve, slant
Retrace, curve forward
and back

Undercurve, slant
Retrace, curve
forward, loop
Curve forward
and back
Retrace, curve right

Undercurve, slant
Retrace, curve forward
and back
Curve forward,
undercurve

MODEL THE WRITING

Model each letter and say the stroke descriptions, emphasizing the undercurve-slant in each. Ask questions such as these:
Which letters curve forward and back to the slant stroke?
Which letter curves forward and loops?
How many retraces does each letter have?
(visual, auditory)

EVALUATE

To help students evaluate their writing, ask questions such as these:
Do your letters have correct slant?
Is each letter about the same width as the model?
Are the forward curves of your **B** parallel with the slant stroke?
(visual, auditory)

Joining Alert

Joining **B** to the letter that follows is optional.

Name

P and *B* are not joined to the letter that follows.
R is joined to the letter that follows.

Write the letters, joinings, and words. Then write the sentences.

P   *P*   *P*   *Phoenix Paddington*

B   *B*   *B*   *Bengal*   *Bataan*

R   *R*   *R*   *Reading*   *Rhodes*

DID YOU KNOW?

Phoenix lies in a valley.

Bataan is a peninsula.

Rhodes is a Greek island.

EVALUATE Circle your best word.

Copyright © Zaner-Bloser, Inc.   **PRACTICE MASTER II**

PRACTICE MASTER II

27

Name the letters with loops (**G, S, L, D**) and the undercurve-slant letters (**P, R, B**). Invite volunteers to write each letter on the chalkboard and answer questions such as these:

Where does your letter begin?

Where does your letter end?

Does your letter have a loop?

Does your letter join to the letter that follows?

COACHING HINT

Students who have mastered the skill of writing the uppercase and lowercase letters without models should be given writing activities that will challenge them and require thinking.

WRITE AWAY

Ask students to choose one of the states shown on page 28, make up a new nickname for it, and write a sentence explaining that nickname. Share an example with students.

Review

Write state nicknames.

Paradise of the Pacific

Gopher State

Land of the Dakotas

Baked Bean State

Little Rhody

On Your Own Write your state's nickname.

EVALUATE Do your letters have correct slant?   Yes   No

Does each $\mathcal{P}$, $\mathcal{R}$, and $\mathcal{B}$ begin with an undercurve?   Yes   No

28

EVALUATE

Guide students through the self-evaluation process, focusing on letter formation and slant. Encourage students to explain why one letter they wrote might be better than another. (visual, auditory)

Manuscript Maintenance

1 A	2 B	3 C	4 D	5 E	6 F	7 G	8 H	9 I	10 J	11 K	12 L	13 M
14 N	15 O	16 P	17 Q	18 R	19 S	20 T	21 U	22 V	23 W	24 X	25 Y	26 Z

Decode each riddle and its answer. Write in uppercase manuscript.

W H A T   D O E S
23 8 1 20   4 15 5 19

D E L A W A R E ?
4 5 12 1 23 1 18 5

A   N E W   J E R S E Y
1   14 5 23   10 5 18 19 5 25

W H E R E   H A S
23 8 5 18 5   8 1 19

O R E G O N ?
15 18 5 7 15 14

T O   O K L A H O M A
20 15   15 11 12 1 8 15 13 1

On Your Own Write a riddle and answer about another state.

_____

_____

EVALUATE Are your letters vertical? Yes No

29

EVALUATE

Have students focus on verticality to determine whether their upper-case manuscript letters are legible. Discuss ways to improve legibility. (visual, auditory)

BEFORE WRITING

Discuss codes with students. Point out that secret codes have existed since earliest times. Tell them the simplest codes involve transposing letters (LHPE for HELP) or substituting other letters, numerals, or symbols for the letters of the alphabet.

MANUSCRIPT MAINTENANCE

Review the keys to legibility for manuscript writing: size and shape, slant, and spacing. Encourage students to follow these suggestions.

• Position the paper correctly.

• Pull the downstrokes in the proper direction.

• Shift the paper as your writing fills the space.

Right-handed students should pull downstrokes toward the midsection. Left-handed students should pull downstrokes toward the left elbow. Guide students in evaluating vertical quality. (visual, auditory, kinesthetic)

COACHING HINT

Practicing pull down straight strokes at the chalkboard is a good way to improve poor strokes. Place sets of two dots about six inches apart to mark the starting and stopping points of each vertical stroke. (visual, kinesthetic)

WRITE AWAY

Challenge students working in pairs to devise their own code and write a riddle and its answer. Have them use pictograms, numerals, letters, or other symbols.

KEYS TO LEGIBILITY: SIZE AND SHAPE

Discuss how both the lowercase and uppercase letters are grouped. Draw attention to the ending stroke of each letter. Model how to join a letter to

- an undercurve
- a downcurve
- an overcurve

Provide opportunities for students to practice the joinings. (visual, auditory, kinesthetic)

COACHING HINT

The joining stroke between letters must be wide enough to allow for good spacing. There should be just enough space for a minimum-sized oval. Have students practice joinings to reinforce both fluent strokes and good spacing. (visual, kinesthetic)

Review Cursive Letters
Write each joining. Then write a word using the joining.

undercurve to undercurve	*ti*
undercurve to downcurve	*pa*
undercurve to overcurve	*in*
overcurve to undercurve	*je*
overcurve to downcurve	*zo*
overcurve to overcurve	*gy*
checkstroke to undercurve	*wh*
checkstroke to downcurve	*ba*
checkstroke to overcurve	*ov*

Write one or two sentences using some of the words you wrote above.

EVALUATE Circle your best joining.
Circle your best word.

30

EVALUATE

Guide students through the self-evaluation process, focusing on joinings. Encourage them to explain why one joining or word they wrote might be better than another. (visual, auditory)

A, C, E, N, M, K, H, U, Y, Z, I, and *R*

are joined to the letter that follows.

O, V, X, W, T, F, I, Q, G, S, L, D, P, and *B*

are not joined to the letter that follows.

Play Geography. Write a list of places. Each place name must begin with the last letter of the previous name. Use state and other place names. Example:

New York, Kalamazoo, Orange County

EVALUATE Circle your best word.

EVALUATE

Guide students through the self-evaluation process, focusing on join-ings. Encourage them to explain why one joining or word they wrote might be better than another. (visual, auditory)

Certificates of Progress *should be awarded to those students who show notable handwriting progress and* Certificates of Excellence *to those who progress to the top levels of handwriting proficiency.*

WRITE AWAY

Ask students to write a list of place names that begin with their first initial. Participate by naming several places that begin with the same letter as your first name.

COACHING HINT

On the chalkboard, write words with several obvious errors in the formation of letters. Have students come to the chalkboard to locate, identify, and cor-rect the errors. (visual, kinesthetic)

Will the real John Hancock sign in please?

Now that you have practiced the letterforms, you are ready to write without models. Write a sentence in cursive.

You'll find that the more you write in cursive, the easier and faster it will be. In the following lessons, you'll write more and learn more about handwriting. You'll focus on size and shape, slant, and spacing to help make your handwriting more legible.

32

UNIT SUMMARY

This page serves as an introduction to Unit 3. The unit is divided into three sections, each having a different handwriting emphasis: (1) size and shape, (2) slant, and (3) spacing. The lessons in each section provide opportunities for meaningful practice and application of handwriting skills in a variety of formats. Evaluations focus on the keys to legibility. The primary goal is for students to develop speed and fluency in cursive writing.

PREVIEW THE UNIT

Preview the unit with students, calling attention to these features:
• timed writing exercises
• everyday writing applications
• proofreading practice
• creative writing assignments
• study of handwriting
• writing in other languages
• manuscript maintenance

Also call attention to these page features:
• writing models
• hints for writing legibly
• writing extensions
• opportunities to evaluate legibility
• facts about people, places, and things

Keys to Legibility: Size and Shape

LEGIBLE LETTERS

Remember! Tall letters should not touch the headline.
Short letters should be half the height of tall letters.
Descenders should not go too far below the baseline.

Aa Bb Cc Dd Ee Ff Gg
Hh Ii Jj Kk Ll Mm
Nn Oo Pp Qq Rr Ss Tt
Uu Vv Ww Xx Yy Zz
1 2 3 4 5 6 7 8 9 10

Write the uppercase letters.

_____

_____

Write the tall lowercase letters.

_____

Write the short lowercase letters.

_____

_____

Write the letters with descenders.

_____

Write the numerals I through 10.

_____

EVALUATE

Are all your tall letters the same size?	Yes	No
Are all your short letters the same size?	Yes	No
Are your numerals the same height as tall letters?	Yes	No

33

MODEL THE WRITING

Model writing a tall letter, a short letter, and a letter with a descender, noting the placement of each letter on the guidelines. Remind students that all letters of the same size should be the same height. (visual, auditory)

EVALUATE

Guide students through the self-evaluation process. Then ask if they can read their letters and numerals easily. Encourage them to explain why or why not. (visual, auditory)

BEFORE WRITING

Remind students that the word *cursive* comes from the Latin *currere*, which means "to run." Cursive was developed as a faster way to write. Poll students to find out how many can write in cursive more quickly than they can in manuscript. Tell students they will be completing a timed writing exercise to find out how quickly and legibly they can write in cursive. Ask them to keep this page in their books or writing portfolios for comparison with page 58 later in the year.

KEYS TO LEGIBILITY: SIZE AND SHAPE

Remind students that all letters of the same size should be even in height and that descenders should not go too far below the baseline. Point out that smooth handwriting is a result of *writing* letters, not drawing them. Provide opportunities to practice letters and joinings on guidelines. (visual, auditory, kinesthetic)

WRITE AWAY

Ask students to write a paragraph explaining the meaning of the sentence they wrote on page 34 and telling how it might apply to a particular experience in their lives. Participate by sharing the meaning of a favorite saying of your own.

COACHING HINT

Writing rate will increase as students begin to move the writing hand more freely. Have students practice writing letters and words in large size with crayon on folded newsprint to overcome finger motion. (kinesthetic)

Write Quickly

Practice writing quickly. Choose one of these sayings from Ben Franklin's *Poor Richard's Almanack* or a favorite saying of your own. Write the sentence as many times as you can in one minute. At the same time, try to write legibly.

Fish and visitors smell in three days.
If your head is wax, don't walk in the sun.
A small leak will sink a great ship.

LEGIBLE LETTERS

Do not draw your letters.
Write smoothly.

EVALUATE Can you read your writing easily?   Yes   No
Can a friend read it?   Yes   No

34

EVALUATE

Help students determine whether writing quickly has affected the size and shape of their letters. Suggest they choose a word that needs improvement and have them practice the letters and joinings in that word. (visual, auditory)

Write a Business Letter

Read this business letter. Notice its six parts.

320 North Stuart Street
Winchester, Virginia 22601 ← **heading**
December 5, 19 ___

New York Public Library
5th Avenue and 42nd Street ← **inside address**
New York, New York 10018-2188

Dear Librarian: ← **salutation**
    I understand you have one of the world's
largest autograph collections. I will be in New York ← **body**
City in March. Could you send me information
about visiting your collection?

    Thank you.

                    Sincerely, ← **closing**

                    Anina Williams ← **signature**

Write the body of Anina's letter or of a business letter of your own.
Pay attention to the size and shape of your letters.

_____

_____

_____

_____

_____

_____

_____

EVALUATE Are your short letters half the height of your tall letters?   Yes   No

35

EVALUATE

After students have evaluated the size of their letters, ask if their writing is legible. Ask them to explain why or why not. (visual, auditory)

BEFORE WRITING

Talk about philography—the hobby of collecting autographs. Ask what kinds of autographs students collect or would like to collect. Point out that some autographs are valuable. For example, in 1986 someone paid $360,000 for a letter with Thomas Jefferson's signature.

WRITE AWAY

Suggest students write a letter requesting an autograph of a favorite author, politician, actor, or sports hero. Help students locate the address of the celebrity. Remind them to use business letter form. Ask students to bring to class an envelope to be addressed after they have completed page 36.

Practice Masters 46–53 provide practice in writing across the curriculum.

BEFORE WRITING

Share with students several business envelopes from banks, utility companies, publishing houses, and so on. If possible, also show students envelopes addressed using calligraphy. Discuss the importance of addressing envelopes legibly.

KEYS TO LEGIBILITY: SIZE AND SHAPE

Provide opportunities for students to practice cursive numerals and punctuation marks on guidelines. (visual, auditory, kinesthetic)

WRITE AWAY

Have students address envelopes for the letters they wrote on page 35. Before stamping and mailing the envelopes, have students work in pairs to evaluate legibility.

Address an Envelope

When you address an envelope, include a return address as well as a mailing address.

Anina Williams
320 North Stuart Street
Winchester, Virginia 22601   return address

New York Public Library
5th Avenue and 42nd Street   mailing address
New York, New York 10018-2788

Address the envelope. Use the return and mailing addresses above or two addresses of your own. Adjust the size of your writing to fit the writing space.

LEGIBLE LETTERS   Remember! Numerals are the same height as tall letters.

EVALUATE   Ask a friend to read and evaluate your writing.
Are the addresses legible?   Yes   No

36

EVALUATE

Pair students and have them discuss the legibility of their envelopes. Encourage students to make suggestions for improving legibility. (visual, auditory)

Write Punctuation Marks

Use these punctuation marks to help clarify your writing.

. period	? question mark	! exclamation point
, comma	' apostrophe	" " quotation marks

Write each sentence in cursive. Remember to slant punctuation marks.

"I'm thirsty." Sarah whined.

"She's bothering me!" Sam complained.

"Settle down back there!" Dad ordered.

"Are we there yet?" I asked.

On Your Own Write a sentence with at least three punctuation marks.

EVALUATE Are your question mark and exclamation point the correct size?   Yes   No

37

EVALUATE

After students have evaluated their punctuation marks, ask if their writing is legible. Ask them to explain why or why not. (visual, auditory)

BEFORE WRITING

Discuss with students how punctuation marks help clarify meaning. Write the following sentence on the chalkboard: *Judy said Ralph let's go.* Have a volunteer punctuate the sentence so that Judy is speaking to Ralph. Then ask a second student to write the sentence, punctuating it so that Ralph is speaking to Judy.

WRITE AWAY

Ask students to write the same sentence twice, punctuating it a different way each time to show a different meaning. Have volunteers write their sentences on the chalkboard without punctuation marks. Classmates can add punctuation marks to show meaning.

COACHING HINT

Correct body position influences smoothness. Encourage students to sit comfortably erect, with their feet flat on the floor and their hips touching the back of the chair. Both arms rest on the desk. The elbows are off the desk. (kinesthetic)

BEFORE WRITING

Ask students if they have ever followed a dirt road or path just to see where it went. Invite students to share their experiences.

KEYS TO LEGIBILITY: SIZE AND SHAPE

Remind students to shift words with ascenders so they do not collide with descenders above them. Provide practice in writing tall letters below letters with descenders. (visual, auditory, kinesthetic)

Write About a Photograph

Imagine you are on this road. Think about it and answer the questions.

Where Have You Been?

Where Are You Now?

Where Are You Going?

38

EVALUATE

Ask students to evaluate the legibility of their charts, reminding them that the charts are for their own use. Suggest that students cross out and rewrite any words they might find hard to read later. (visual, auditory, kinesthetic)

Write about your journey in your travel diary. Tell what you found at the end of the road.

COLLISION
ALERT   Make sure your tall letters do not bump into the descenders above them.

_____

_____

_____

_____

_____

_____

_____

_____

_____

_____

_____

_____

_____

EVALUATE Did you avoid collisions?   Yes   No
              Is your writing legible?   Yes   No

EVALUATE

After students have evaluated the legibility of their writing, discuss "bumping." Ask what they did to avoid collisions. Encourage students to practice writing words with tall letters beneath words with descenders, shifting words slightly if necessary. (visual, auditory, kinesthetic)

WRITE AWAY

Have students compile a list of titles for the picture on page 38. Suggest several possibilities, such as "Dirt Road" or "In a Rut?"

COACHING HINT

On the chalkboard, demonstrate the letters with descenders. Have students trace the descending stroke with colored chalk to highlight its shape and size. (visual, kinesthetic)

BEFORE WRITING

Discuss writing systems with students. Point out that we use the Roman alphabet, a writing system of 26 letters based on sounds. Other writing systems, such as Japanese, are based on syllables or words. With 74 letters, the Cambodian alphabet is the world's longest. With 11 letters, an alphabet from the Easter Islands is the world's shortest.

WRITE AWAY

Ask students to use an encyclopedia or other reference sources to research another alphabet and write a brief report on it. Alphabets that might interest students include Arabic, Cree, Hebrew, Chinese, and Cyrillic.

COACHING HINT

Draw writing lines on one side of 9" x 12" pieces of oak tag, and laminate one piece for each student. Students can use these as "slates" and practice their handwriting with a wipe-off marker. The reverse side can be used for letter activities. (visual, kinesthetic)

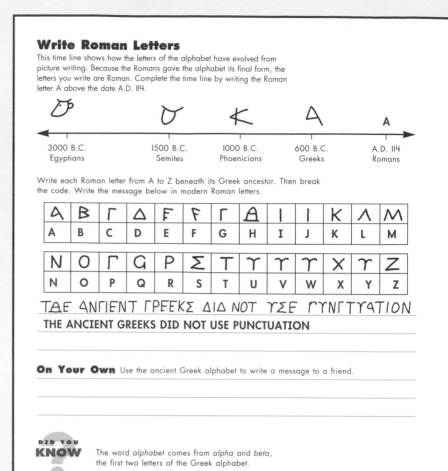

Write Roman Letters

This time line shows how the letters of the alphabet have evolved from picture writing. Because the Romans gave the alphabet its final form, the letters you write are Roman. Complete the time line by writing the Roman letter A above the date A.D. 114.

| 3000 B.C. | 1500 B.C. | 1000 B.C. | 600 B.C. | A.D. 114 |
| Egyptians | Semites | Phoenicians | Greeks | Romans |

Write each Roman letter from A to Z beneath its Greek ancestor. Then break the code. Write the message below in modern Roman letters.

A	B	Γ	Δ	F	F	Γ	A	I	I	K	Λ	M
A	B	C	D	E	F	G	H	I	J	K	L	M

N	O	Γ	G	P	Σ	T	Y	Y	Y	X	Y	Z
N	O	P	Q	R	S	T	U	V	W	X	Y	Z

TΔE ΛΝΓIΕΝΤ ΓΡΕΕΚΣ ΔIΔ NOT YΣE ΓYΝΓTYΛTIΟΝ

THE ANCIENT GREEKS DID NOT USE PUNCTUATION

On Your Own Use the ancient Greek alphabet to write a message to a friend.

DID YOU KNOW The word *alphabet* comes from *alpha* and *beta*, the first two letters of the Greek alphabet.

40

EVALUATE

Ask students if they took more care in writing the message to a friend than in decoding the message on the page for themselves. Encourage them to explain why or why not. (visual, auditory)

Write in Spanish

What time is it?	¿Qué hora es?
It is 1:00.	Es la una.
It is 2:00.	Son las dos.
2:15	dos y cuarto
2:30	dos y media
2:45	tres menos cuarto

Write the time in Spanish. Use the word and number keys to help you.

1 una	4 cuatro	7 siete	10 diez
2 dos	5 cinco	8 ocho	11 once
3 tres	6 seis	9 nueve	12 doce

1. **6:00**   2. **5:15**   3. **7:45**   4. **11:15**   5. **10:30**

1. *Son las seis.*
2. Son las cinco y cuarto.
3. Son las ocho menos cuarto.
4. Son las once y cuarto.
5. Son las diez y media.

On Your Own ¿Qué hora es? Answer in Spanish to the nearest quarter hour.

_____

EVALUATE Are all your short letters the same size? Yes No

EVALUATE

After students have evaluated the size of their letters, ask if their writing is legible. Ask them to explain why or why not. (visual, auditory)

¿Qué hora es? (keh OH rah ehs)
Es la una. (ehs lah OO nah)
Son las dos. (sohn lahs dohs)
dos y cuarto (dohs ee KWAHR toh)
dos y media (dohs ee MEH dee=ah)
tres menos cuarto (trehs MEH nohs KWAHR toh)

una (OO nah)
dos (DOHS)
tres (TREHS)
cuatro (KWAH troh)
cinco (SEEN koh)
seis (SEH=EES)
siete (SEE=EH teh)
ocho (OH choh)
nueve (NOO=EH veh)
diez (DEE=ehs)
once (OHN seh)
doce (DOH seh)

BEFORE WRITING

Ask students what languages they know besides English. Discuss the advantages of knowing a second language. Invite a Spanish-speaking student to read aloud the Spanish words and expressions on the page.

KEYS TO LEGIBILITY: SIZE AND SHAPE

Invite volunteers to demonstrate the technique of drawing a horizontal line with a ruler along the tops of their letters to show proper size. (visual, kinesthetic)

WRITE AWAY

Have students choose a topic, such as meeting people or traveling by car, and compile a list of useful English words and phrases for students of English as a second language. Students who speak Spanish might write lists of Spanish words.

Practice Masters 27–45 provide additional practice in writing in Spanish.

KEYS TO LEGIBILITY: SIZE AND SHAPE

Review the cursive alphabet with students, helping them group the letters according to size.

- Tall letters should not touch the headline. Lowercase **b, d, f, h, k, l,** and **t** are tall. All uppercase letters are tall.

- Short letters are half the height of tall letters. Lowercase **a, c, e, g, i, j, m, n, o, p, q, r, s, u, v, w, x, y,** and **z** are short.

- Letters with descenders extend below the baseline. Lowercase **f, g, j, p, q, y,** and **z** have descenders. Uppercase **J, Y,** and **Z** have descenders.

Provide opportunities to practice proper placement of each letter on handwriting guidelines. (visual, auditory, kinesthetic)

WRITE AWAY

Point out that "Michael Finnegan" is a circular song. Invite students to work in small groups to write their own circular songs.

COACHING HINT

Right-handed teachers will better understand the stroke, visual perspective, and posture of the left-handed student if they practice the left-handed position themselves.

Evaluate Size and Shape

Michael Finnegan

There was an old man
named Michael Finnegan.
He had whiskers on his chinnegan.
Along came the wind and
blew them in again.
Poor old Michael Finnegan.
Begin again.

Write this American folk song in your best handwriting. Pay special attention to the size and shape of your letters.

EVALUATE		
Are your tall letters all the same size?	Yes	No
Are your short letters half the height of your tall letters?	Yes	No
Did you avoid collisions?	Yes	No

42

EVALUATE

As part of the self-evaluation process, have students focus on size and shape. Ask them to describe ways they might improve their writing. If necessary, have students rewrite the folk song, aiming for their personal best. (visual, auditory)

Certificates of Progress *should be awarded to those students who show notable handwriting progress and* Certificates of Excellence *to those who progress to the top levels of handwriting proficiency.*

Keys to Legibility: Uniform Slant

Follow these suggestions to write with uniform slant.

POSITION   Check your paper position.
PULL   Pull your downstrokes in the proper direction.
SHIFT   Shift your paper as you write.

If you are left-handed . . .   **If you are right-handed . . .**

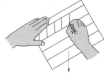

pull toward your left elbow.   pull toward your midsection.

Write the titles of these American folk songs. Try to make your slant uniform.

"Yankee Doodle"

"Jennie Jenkins"

"John Henry"

"Mrs. Murphy's Chowder"

EVALUATE   Check your slant.
Draw lines through the slant strokes of the letters.
Your slant should look like ///// , not //// .

43

MODEL THE WRITING

Remind students that, in cursive writing, letters slant to the right. Show an example of correct slant by writing *uniform* on guidelines. Invite a student to check the slant of your writing by drawing lines through the slant strokes of the letters. These lines should slant forward and be parallel. (visual, auditory, kinesthetic)

EVALUATE

Guide students through the self-evaluation process. Then ask if the titles students wrote are easy to read. Encourage students to explain why or why not. (visual, auditory)

BEFORE WRITING

It may interest students to know that all states have, or have had, a number of unusual laws. Among them are *blue laws*, or *Sabbath laws*. Blue laws were the first printed laws of the New Haven Colony in Connecticut. In addition to laws prohibiting business or recreation on Sunday, the following example is listed in *A General History of Connecticut*: "Every male shall have his hair cut round according to a cap."

KEYS TO LEGIBILITY: UNIFORM SLANT

Review the hints for writing with uniform slant (POSITION, PULL, SHIFT). Help students position their papers correctly and check the direction of their strokes. (visual, auditory, kinesthetic)

WRITE AWAY

Ask students to list appropriate penalties for breaking the laws listed on page 44. For example, people who sneeze in public must pay for boxes of tissues to be made available to passersby.

Take Notes

When you take notes from a book, record the title and author. Then write important or interesting information in your own words.

The Kids' World Almanac of the United States by J. G. Aylesworth
Old laws
DC—illegal to punch a bull in the nose
Hawaii—illegal to put pennies in your ears

Take notes on the following paragraph from *Blue Laws and True Laws* by I.B. Sofer. As you write, pay attention to slant.

There are some unusual laws that are still on the books in the United States. So if you're in a public eating place in New Jersey, don't slurp your soup. If you're in Pittsburgh, don't push dirt under a rug. Don't wipe dishes dry in Minneapolis. It's against the law!

EVALUATE Can you read your notes easily?   Yes   No
             Will you be able to read your notes next week?   Yes   No

EVALUATE

Ask students how slant affects the legibility of their writing. Suggest they check the slant of a word by drawing lines through the slant strokes. Encourage them to practice pulling downstrokes in the proper direction. (visual, auditory, kinesthetic)

Write a Paragraph

The following sentences tell about the Smithsonian Institution in Washington, D.C. Write the sentences in the correct order to make a good paragraph. Begin with the sentence that states the main idea.

Its thirteen museums are crammed with more than 100 million objects. From Teddy Roosevelt's own teddy bear to a live scorpion the size of a crab, you're bound to find something interesting to see. It's no wonder the Smithsonian is called "America's attic."

POSITION
PULL
SHIFT

Remember! Check the way you position your paper and the direction you pull the downstrokes.

It's no wonder the Smithsonian is called "America's attic." Its

thirteen museums are crammed with more than 100 million objects.

From Teddy Roosevelt's own teddy bear to a live scorpion the size

of a crab, you're bound to find something interesting to see.

EVALUATE Draw lines through the slant strokes in your letters. Is your slant uniform?   Yes   No

DID YOU
KNOW

Washington, D.C., is a city without a state.

45

EVALUATE

After students have evaluated their slant, have them describe what they did to make their slant uniform. Ask if their writing is legible, and have them explain why or why not. (visual, auditory)

BEFORE WRITING

Ask how many students have visited the Smithsonian Institution in Washington, D.C. Point out that the museum houses 77 spacecraft, 12 million postage stamps, 35,594 skeletons, 30,834 costumes, 6,214 African masks, 4,500 meteorites, and many other things.

WRITE AWAY

Ask students to write a paragraph about an item they would contribute to the Smithsonian. In their paragraphs, students should explain what makes their proposed contribution valuable. Participate by suggesting an item you might contribute.

Practice Masters 46–53 provide practice in writing across the curriculum.

COACHING HINT

Holding the writing instrument correctly has an obvious effect on handwriting quality. Students having difficulty with the conventional method of holding the writing instrument may wish to try an alternate method: placing the pen or pencil between the first and second fingers. (kinesthetic)

BEFORE WRITING

Discuss the role of editing and the use of proofreading marks in the writing process. On the chalkboard, write several sentences with various errors. Demonstrate how to use the proofreading marks to show the errors.

KEYS TO LEGIBILITY: UNIFORM SLANT

Evaluate slant by drawing lines through the slant strokes of the letters. The lines should be parallel and should show uniform forward slant. (visual, kinesthetic)

WRITE AWAY

Ask students to compile a list of additional "rules" for museum-goers. Students should include rules that will ensure they have fun at the museum, for example, "Strike a pose next to your favorite statue, and ask someone to take your picture."

Edit Your Writing

Use these proofreading marks to edit your writing.

≡ Capitalize.	∧ Insert (add).
/ Use lowercase.	⅍ Delete (take out).
⊙ Add period.	⇶ Indent for paragraph.

Write this paragraph correctly. Make the changes indicated by the proofreading marks.

¶ ~~Your~~ Anyone can have a good time at a museum. Just follow ~~the~~ these Rules. Eat something ~~food~~ before you go. wear comfortable shoes. Don't try to see everything! Just pick one or two exhibits that interest you⊙

_____

_____

_____

_____

_____

_____

_____

EVALUATE Does your writing have uniform slant?   Yes   No

EVALUATE

After students have evaluated their slant, ask if their writing is legible. Have them explain why or why not. (visual, auditory)

Manuscript Maintenance

Fill out the conference registration form below. Use the information that follows or information that you supply. Please print.

Zach Tyler
2500 Dearborn Avenue
Skokie, Illinois 60076
School: Pierce Middle School
Grade: 5
Book Title: I Can Draw
Book Description: This is a how-to book with directions for using a compass to draw geometric designs.

Young Authors' Roundtable

[ ] YES! I would like to attend the Young Authors' Roundtable
at the City Civic Center on May 25, 199____.

_____
NAME (Please print.)

_____
ADDRESS

_____
CITY   STATE   ZIP

_____
SCHOOL   GRADE

What is the title of the book you have written?
_____

Write a short description of your book.
_____
_____
_____

EVALUATE Ask a friend to read and evaluate your writing.
Is the completed application legible?   Yes   No

47

EVALUATE

Pair students and have them discuss the legibility of their application forms. Encourage students to make suggestions for improving legibility. (visual, auditory)

BEFORE WRITING

Share with students a variety of forms, including contest entry forms, magazine subscription forms, and catalog order forms. Discuss what the forms have in common.

MANUSCRIPT MAINTENANCE

Remind students that manuscript writing is vertical. To achieve verticality, right-handed students should pull the downstrokes toward the midsection. Left-handed students should pull the downstrokes toward the left elbow. Ask students to write their names in manuscript. Guide them in evaluating vertical quality. (visual, auditory, kinesthetic)

The form on page 47 is reproduced on Practice Master 12.

WRITE AWAY

Ask students to use manuscript writing to design forms for various uses in the classroom. Students can then trade and complete forms.

COACHING HINT

Write the same word on the chalkboard in cursive and in manuscript. Use parallel lines of colored chalk to highlight the difference between manuscript verticality and cursive slant.

BEFORE WRITING

Share the following information with students: "Spoonbridge and Cherry," designed by Claes Oldenburg and Coosje van Bruggen, is 52 feet long and 29 feet high. The sculpture is a working fountain. Water flows from both the base of the cherry and the top of the stem.

KEYS TO LEGIBILITY: UNIFORM SLANT

Most errors in slant can be corrected in one of the following ways:

1. Check paper position.

2. Pull the downstrokes in the proper direction.

3. Shift the paper as the writing progresses across the line. (visual, kinesthetic)

Write About a Sculpture

Spoonbridge and Cherry, 1985-988 Aluminum, Stainless Steel, Paint (354 x 618 x 162")
by C. Oldenburg and C. van Bruggen
Collection Walker Art Center, Minneapolis.
Gift of Frederick R. Weisman in honor of his parents, William and Mary Weisman, 1988.

This sculpture in the Minneapolis Sculpture Garden is called "Spoonbridge and Cherry." Look at it carefully and answer the questions.

What Do You See?	Where Do You See It?

48

EVALUATE

Ask students to evaluate the legibility of their charts, reminding them that the charts are for their own use. Suggest that students cross out and rewrite any words they might find hard to read later. (visual, auditory, kinesthetic)

Write a paragraph telling a friend about the sculpture. Include details that will help your friend form a mental picture of it.

LEGIBLE LETTERS

Slant strokes in letters should be parallel.

_____
_____
_____
_____
_____
_____
_____
_____
_____
_____
_____
_____
_____
_____
_____

EVALUATE Ask a friend to read and evaluate your writing.
Is the slant uniform?   Yes   No
Is the paragraph legible?   Yes   No

49

WRITE AWAY

Ask students to write a paragraph about an imaginary sculpture. Then have pairs of students exchange paragraphs and draw their partner's sculpture based on the description.

COACHING HINT

To help students improve slant, draw parallel slant lines and have a student change them into the slant strokes of a word. (visual, kinesthetic)

EVALUATE

Pair students and have them discuss how slant affects the legibility of their writing. Suggest students look at the slant of one group of letters in their words (for example, undercurve letters) and check if the slant is uniform. Encourage students to write several rows of any troublesome letters, using the hints for writing with uniform slant. (visual, auditory, kinesthetic)

BEFORE WRITING

Write your signature on the chalkboard. Point out that a person's signature is an important and personal part of writing. Since no two people are alike, each person's signature is unique. Discuss how personality can affect the way a person signs his or her name.

WRITE AWAY

Ask students to write a paragraph analyzing their signatures. In their paragraphs, students should tell what they think their signatures reveal about them.

COACHING HINT

Correct paper placement is a factor in legibility. Remind students to check this periodically. (kinesthetic)

Write Your Signature

As president of the Continental Congress in 1776, John Hancock signed the Declaration of Independence with a flourish. Circle the bold signature for which Hancock became famous.

Experiment with your signature. Write your initials, your nickname, your full name, and any other form of your name that you like. Write in manuscript and cursive, with large letters and small letters.

Write your name as if you were signing the Declaration of Independence.

EVALUATE Circle the signature that shows the real you.

DID YOU KNOW ? *Put your John Hancock here* means "Write your signature."

EVALUATE

Ask students if their signatures are legible. Ask them to explain why or why not. (visual, auditory)

Evaluate Slant

Oh, Susannah

I came from Salem City
with my washpan on my knee.
I'm going to California.
The gold dust for to see.
It rained all night the day I left.
The weather it was dry.
The sun so hot I froze to death.
Oh, brothers, don't you cry!

Write these lines from an American folk song in your best handwriting.
Pay special attention to slant.

_____

_____

_____

_____

_____

_____

_____

_____

_____

EVALUATE Does your writing have uniform slant? Yes No

51

KEYS TO LEGIBILITY: UNIFORM SLANT

Remind students that in cursive writing all letters slant to the right. Review the hints for writing with uniform slant for both left-handed and right-handed writers.

- Position your paper correctly.
- Pull the downstrokes in the proper direction.
- Shift your paper to the left as you write.

Invite both left-handed and right-handed students to model for classmates. (visual, auditory, kinesthetic)

WRITE AWAY

Ask students to revise the first stanza of "Oh, Susannah" to tell a modern-day story about someone moving from one part of the country to another. Participate by sharing an opening line, such as "I came from Texarkana, a computer in my bag."

EVALUATE

Guide students through the self-evaluation process, focusing on slant. Ask students whether improvement is needed. If necessary, have students rewrite the folk song, aiming for their personal best. (visual, auditory)

Certificates of Progress *should be awarded to those students who show notable handwriting progress and* Certificates of Excellence *to those who progress to the top levels of handwriting proficiency.*

Keys to Legibility: Correct Spacing

These sentences are legible. The spacing is correct.

Between Letters There should be space for *a*
Between Words There should be space for ╲ *o*
Between Sentences There should be space for *O.*

to see. O It rained

Write these lines from the song "Oh, Susannah" in paragraph form.
For correct spacing, shift your paper as you write.

I soon shall be in Frisco and there I'll look around. And when I see the gold lumps there, I'll pick them off the ground.

EVALUATE Is there space for *O* between letters?   Yes   No

Is there space for ╲ between words?   Yes   No

Is there space for *O* between sentences?   Yes   No

52

MODEL THE WRITING

To show an example of correct spacing, write the following sentences on guidelines: *Don't you cry for me. I'm going to California.* Invite volunteers to check the spacing by drawing ovals between letters, by drawing slanted lines between words, and by writing uppercase **O** between sentences. (visual, auditory, kinesthetic)

EVALUATE

Guide students through the self-evaluation process. Then ask if their sentences are easy to read. Encourage students to explain why or why not. (visual, auditory)

Write Lead Sentences

A lead sentence is the first sentence of a story. It may tell *who, what, when,* and *where.* Sometimes it tells *why.*

James Wilson Marshall *discovered gold*

   who   what

at Sutter's Mill *this morning.*

  where   when

Use the facts to write lead sentences.

Who: *Mrs. O'Leary's cow*   Where: *in the O'Leary barn*

What: *kicked over a lantern*   When: *last night*

_____

_____

_____

Who: *Abolitionist Sojourner Truth*

What: *spoke*   When: *yesterday*

Where: *at Seneca Falls*   Why: *to get voting rights*

_____

_____

_____

On Your Own Write a lead sentence about either a school event or a historical event. Try to include the five W's: *who, what, when, where,* and *why.*

_____

_____

EVALUATE Is there space for *O* between letters?   Yes No

53

BEFORE WRITING

Share with students lead sentences of articles in a newspaper. Discuss which of the five *W*'s (*who, what, when, where,* and *why*) are covered by the story leads.

KEYS TO LEGIBILITY: CORRECT SPACING

Remind students that shifting their papers as they write can help keep spacing consistent. (visual, kinesthetic)

WRITE AWAY

Ask students to complete the story they began on page 53. Point out that in the process of writing, students may want to revise their story leads.

EVALUATE

After students have evaluated the spacing between their letters, ask if their writing is legible. Have them explain why or why not. (visual, auditory)

BEFORE WRITING

On the chalkboard write these two simple sentences:

Did Benjamin Franklin win the debate?
Did the bald eagle become our national bird?

Demonstrate how to use a comma and the word *or* to combine the sentences.

KEYS TO LEGIBILITY: CORRECT SPACING

Remind students that a little more space is needed before words that begin with a downcurve letter (**a, c, d, q, g, o**). (visual, auditory)

WRITE AWAY

Ask students if they are pleased with the selection of the bald eagle as our national bird. Ask them to write a paragraph in support of the eagle or another bird. Suggest students write a statement of opinion followed by supporting facts.

Write Compound Sentences

Two simple sentences can be combined to form a compound sentence.

Is the bald eagle graceful and powerful, or is it mean and cowardly?

Use a comma and the word in parentheses to combine each pair of sentences.

Ben Franklin wanted the turkey to represent our country.
Congress chose the bald eagle. (but)

_____

_____

Franklin praised the turkey's courage.
He condemned the bald eagle's cowardice. (and)

_____

_____

Is the turkey bold and fierce?
Is it vain and silly? (or)

_____

_____

EVALUATE Is there space for   between words?   Yes   No

54

EVALUATE

After students have evaluated the spacing between their words, ask if their writing is legible. Have them explain why or why not. (visual, auditory)

Manuscript Maintenance

Use an encyclopedia to complete the chart about the North Central States.
Write in manuscript.

LEGIBLE
LETTERS

Write smaller to fit the writing space.

The North Central States

State	Capital	State Song
North Dakota	Bismark	"North Dakota Hymn"
South Dakota	Pierre	"Hail! South Dakota"
Nebraska	Lincoln	"Beautiful Nebraska"
Kansas	Topeka	"Home on the Range"
Minnesota	St. Paul	"Hail! Minnesota"
Iowa	Des Moines	"The Song of Iowa"
Missouri	Jefferson City	"Missouri Waltz"
Wisconsin	Madison	"On, Wisconsin"
Illinois	Springfield	"Illinois"
Michigan	Lansing	"My Michigan"
Ohio	Columbus	"Beautiful Ohio"
Indiana	Indianapolis	"On the Banks of the Wabash,
		Far Away"

EVALUATE Did you adjust your writing to fit the space?   Yes   No
Is the chart legible?   Yes   No

DID YOU
KNOW   "The Star-Spangled Banner" is our national anthem.

EVALUATE

Have students focus on spacing to determine whether their charts
are legible. Discuss how students can improve their spacing. (visual,
auditory)

BEFORE WRITING

On a map of the United States, locate
the North Central States. Ask a volunteer to identify the lakes for which the
region is known (four of the Great
Lakes: Huron, Michigan, Erie, and
Superior).

MANUSCRIPT MAINTENANCE

Review the keys to legibility for manuscript writing: size and shape, slant,
and spacing. Show an example of correct spacing between letters, words,
and sentences. Remind students that letters and words too close together or too
far apart make writing difficult to read.
Provide opportunities for them to practice good spacing. (visual, auditory,
kinesthetic)

WRITE AWAY

Ask students to compile a list of interesting facts about the North Central States,
for example, Minnesota is the home of
the oldest rock. Students can use an
almanac or an encyclopedia as a
source of information.

COACHING HINT

Demonstrate the placement of lightly
drawn lines over manuscript letters as
a check of vertical quality. (visual, auditory, kinesthetic)

BEFORE WRITING

Discuss Thanksgiving with students. Ask what students picture in their minds when they hear the word *Thanksgiving*. Use a word web to record students' responses.

KEYS TO LEGIBILITY: CORRECT SPACING

Remind students there should be enough space for ⊘ between letters, \ between words, and ◯ between sentences. (visual, auditory)

Write About a Painting

Join artist Doris Lee in celebrating Thanksgiving. Step into Doris Lee's "Thanksgiving" and brainstorm words to describe the experience.

Thanksgiving, 1935 Oil on Canvas (71.4 x 101.6cm), by Doris Lee (1905-1983)
Photograph © 1994, The Art Institute of Chicago, Mr. & Mrs. Frank G. Logan Prize Fund. All Rights Reserved.

What I Touch

Doris Lee's "Thanksgiving"

What I See   What I Taste

What I Smell

What I Hear

56

EVALUATE

Ask students to evaluate the legibility of their brainstorming notes, reminding them that the notes are for their own use. Suggest that students cross out and rewrite any words they might find hard to read later. (visual, auditory, kinesthetic)

The art world wants to know! Write about spending Thanksgiving with artist Doris Lee. Write in the first person, using the pronoun *I*.

LEGIBLE LETTERS

Shift your paper as you write.

_____
_____
_____
_____
_____
_____
_____
_____
_____
_____
_____
_____
_____
_____
_____

EVALUATE Is your spacing correct?   Yes   No
Is the paragraph legible?   Yes   No

DID YOU KNOW   In 1789 George Washington proclaimed November 26 a day of national thanksgiving.

57

WRITE AWAY

Ask students to write a short description of the first Thanksgiving. Students can use an encyclopedia or other reference source for information. Participate by sharing the following facts: The first Thanksgiving meal was a breakfast. Native Americans brought turkeys, pumpkins, corn, sweet potatoes, and cranberries to the celebration. Boiled eel, lobster, roast pigeon, and stuffed cod were also served.

COACHING HINT

An occasional check for correct paper and pencil positions is important to maintain good handwriting skills and to help with legibility. (visual, auditory, kinesthetic)

EVALUATE

After students have evaluated their writing, ask if they took more care in writing their paragraphs than in taking notes on page 56. Discuss why or why not. (visual, auditory)

BEFORE WRITING

Remind students that on page 34 they completed a timed writing exercise to find out how quickly and legibly they could write. The writing exercise on this page will enable students to evaluate their progress.

KEYS TO LEGIBILITY: CORRECT SPACING

Remind students that shifting their papers as they write can help keep spacing consistent. (auditory, kinesthetic)

WRITE AWAY

Ask students to write three interesting sayings or idiomatic expressions. Suggest they use a book of proverbs or an almanac as a source of expressions. Participate by sharing these idioms: *Where six can eat, seven can eat* (Spanish); *You can't dance at two weddings at the same time* (Yiddish).

Write Quickly

Practice writing quickly. Choose one of these sayings from Ben Franklin's *Poor Richard's Almanack* or a favorite saying of your own. Write the sentence as many times as you can in one minute. At the same time, try to write legibly.

The cat in gloves catches no mice.
A lie stands on one leg, truth on two.
The honey is sweet, but the bee has a sting.

LEGIBLE LETTERS Do not draw your letters. Write smoothly.

EVALUATE Can you read your writing easily?   Yes   No
Can a friend read it?   Yes   No

58

EVALUATE

Have students determine whether writing quickly has affected legibility. Suggest they compare this writing with their writing on page 34 to see if they are writing more quickly and legibly. (visual, auditory)

Write in French

What time is it?	*Quelle heure est-il?*
It is …	*Il est …*
1:00	*une heure*
2:00	*deux heures*
2:15	*deux heures et quart*
2:30	*deux heures et demie*
2:45	*trois heures moins*
	le quart

Write the time in French. Use the word and number keys to help you.

1 un	*4 quatre*	*7 sept*	*10 dix*
2 deux	*5 cinq*	*8 huit*	*11 onze*
3 trois	*6 six*	*9 neuf*	*12 douze*

1. **6:00**   2. **5:15**   3. **7:45**   4. **11:15**   5. **10:30**

1. *Il est six heures.*
2. Il est cinq heures et quart.
3. Il est huit heures moins le quart.
4. Il est onze heures et quart.
5. Il est dix heures et demie.

On Your Own Quelle heure est-il? Answer in French to the nearest quarter hour.

EVALUATE Is your spacing correct?   Yes   No

59

59

BEFORE WRITING

Show students how to transform their own cursive handwriting into beautiful lettering. Have them write their names, twice as large as usual, in cursive. Instruct them to shade or thicken all the downstrokes, using pencil, marker, crayon, or pastels.

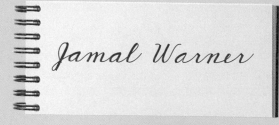

WRITE AWAY

Ask students to write their favorite quotation, using calligraphy or another style of handwriting, such as bold letters, block letters, bubble letters, or stencilled letters.

COACHING HINT

For calligraphy, the pen should be held at a 45° angle. It should be pulled, not pushed, when forming the various strokes. For example, a circle is formed by connecting two pull-down curve strokes. (visual, auditory, kinesthetic)

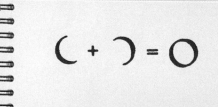

Write Calligraphy

Calligraphy is the art of beautiful handwriting. Here are several systems of calligraphy.

The Chancery Italic Hand

𝕿𝖍𝖊 𝕲𝖔𝖙𝖍𝖎𝖈 𝕳𝖆𝖓𝖉

THE UNCIAL HAND

Try your hand at calligraphy. Use a calligraphy pen or felt-tip marker with a square point. Write these strokes.

Now design your own alphabet.

Use your alphabet to write the name of your system.

EVALUATE

Ask students to discuss what they did to make their writing beautiful. (visual, auditory)

Evaluate Spacing

'Twas Midnight

'Twas midnight on the ocean.
Not a streetcar was in sight.
The sun was shining brightly.
For it rained all day that night.
'Twas a summer day in winter
And snow was raining fast.
As a barefoot boy with shoes on
Stood sitting in the grass.

Write this American folk rhyme in your best handwriting.
Pay special attention to spacing.

_____
_____
_____
_____
_____
_____
_____
_____
_____

EVALUATE Is there space for $\mathcal{O}$ between letters? Yes No

Is there space for \ between words? Yes No

61

61

KEYS TO LEGIBILITY: CORRECT SPACING

Display an example of correct spacing between letters, words, and sentences.

Between Letters There should be enough space for $\mathcal{O}$.

Between Words There should be enough space for \.

Between Sentences There should be enough space for $\mathcal{O}$.

Provide opportunities for students to write two or more sentences and to check the spacing between letters, words, and sentences. (auditory, visual, kinesthetic)

WRITE AWAY

"'Twas Midnight" has been called an "upside-down, inside-out" poem. Ask students to write their own version of the poem by replacing key words with their opposites or near opposites. Students can begin: "'Twas noontime on the desert/Not a paddleboat was in sight."

EVALUATE

Guide students through the self-evaluation process, focusing on spacing. Ask students whether or not improvement is needed. If necessary, have them rewrite the rhyme, aiming for their personal best. (visual, auditory)

Certificates of Progress *should be awarded to those students who show notable handwriting progress and Certificates of Excellence to those who progress to the top levels of handwriting proficiency.*

POSTTEST

Remind students that on page 5, as a pretest, they wrote the first stanza of this folk song and evaluated their handwriting. They will write the same stanza for the posttest. Tell them to use correct letter size and shape, uniform slant, and correct spacing as they write. (visual, auditory, kinesthetic)

Posttest
This Land Is Your Land

This land is your land, this land is my land
From California to the New York island,
From the redwood forest to the Gulf Stream waters
This land was made for you and me.

As I was walking that ribbon of highway,
I saw above me that endless skyway,
I saw below me that golden valley
This land was made for you and me.

Woody Guthrie

On your paper, write the first stanza of this American folk song in your best cursive writing.

EVALUATE Is your writing legible?   Yes   No

62

EVALUATE

Have students use the keys to legibility to evaluate their handwriting. Suggest they compare this writing with their writing on the pretest. Discuss how their writing has changed. Meet individually with students to help them assess their progress. (visual, auditory)

Record of Student's Handwriting Skills

Cursive

	Needs Improvement	Shows Mastery
Sits correctly	☐	☐
Holds pencil correctly	☐	☐
Positions paper correctly	☐	☐
Writes numerals 1–10	☐	☐
Writes undercurve letters: **i, t, u, w**	☐	☐
Writes undercurve letters: **r, s, p, j**	☐	☐
Writes downcurve letters: **a, c, d, q, g, o**	☐	☐
Writes overcurve letters: **n, m, x, y, z, v**	☐	☐
Writes letters with loops: **e, l, h, k, f, b**	☐	☐
Writes downcurve letters: **A, C, E, O**	☐	☐
Writes curve forward letters: **N, M, K, H**	☐	☐
Writes curve forward letters: **U, Y, Z, V, X, W**	☐	☐
Writes doublecurve letters: **T, F**	☐	☐
Writes overcurve letters: **I, Q, J**	☐	☐
Writes letters with loops: **G, S, L, D**	☐	☐
Writes undercurve-slant letters: **P, B, R**	☐	☐
Writes the undercurve to undercurve joining	☐	☐
Writes the undercurve to downcurve joining	☐	☐
Writes the undercurve to overcurve joining	☐	☐
Writes the overcurve to undercurve joining	☐	☐
Writes the overcurve to downcurve joining	☐	☐
Writes the overcurve to overcurve joining	☐	☐
Writes the checkstroke to undercurve joining	☐	☐
Writes the checkstroke to downcurve joining	☐	☐
Writes the checkstroke to overcurve joining	☐	☐
Writes with correct size and shape	☐	☐
Writes with uniform slant	☐	☐
Writes with correct spacing	☐	☐
Writes quickly	☐	☐

63

The form on page 63 is reproduced on Practice Master 13.

COACHING HINT

If a student needs improvement, reevaluate his or her writing following practice over a period of time. Invite the student to share in the evaluation. (visual, auditory)

EVALUATE

This chart provides a place for you to record the student's handwriting progress. The chart lists the essential skills in the program. After each skill has been practiced and evaluated, you can indicate whether the student *Shows Mastery* or *Needs Improvement* by checking the appropriate box.

Shows Mastery Mastery of written letterforms is achieved when the student writes the letters using correct basic strokes. Compare the student's written letterforms with the letter models. Keep in mind the keys to legibility (size and shape, slant, and spacing) when evaluating letters, numerals, punctuation marks, words, and sentences.

Needs Improvement If a student has not mastered a skill, provide additional basic instruction and practice. To improve letterforms, have the student practice writing the letter in isolation and within words and sentences. Reinforce instruction through activities geared to the student's modality strengths. When mastery of the skill is achieved, check *Shows Mastery*.

Index